Praise for **Limitless Future**

"I first met Brian in the early 1990s when he began working as a counselor and coach at my school. Brian was polite enough to let me think I was his supervisor. He was always a fierce advocate for all students; I recall his efforts to assist students in getting into classes where some thought they did not belong. *Limitless Future* is a handbook highlighting just how crucial parents (or those in that role) are and can be in shaping a future for children that should be limitless."

—Mike Durso, parent of four, retired high school principal, and former school board president

"*Limitless Future* is an invaluable guide for parents seeking to nurture their child's unique strengths and passions. This book goes beyond assessing academic reputation and provides a framework for fostering creativity, intelligence, and resilience in every child. By emphasizing the importance of building on strengths, offering diverse opportunities, and collaborating with schools, Butler highlights that true success lies in the support and resources we provide. His insights into brain research and the celebration of individual qualities offer a practical approach to unlocking each child's unlimited potential. A must-read for any parent committed to their child's growth and development."

—Bernard Jones, parent of two, retired teacher

"Brian has a brilliant way of mixing his personal experience with years of educational knowledge and wisdom to create an uplifting and informative resource for parents. This socio-educational roadmap will play a pivotal role in informing parents and encouraging children for years to come. I love how he nudges parents to look at their own behaviors and how they influence their children while also providing suggestions for real ways to weave these practices into our everyday lives. As you turn the last page, I am guessing you will want to order a gift copy for all the wonderful parents in your life!"

—Noelle Klein, RN and mom of four

"Brian Butler's *Limitless Future* provides parents with a comprehensive, easy-to-follow guide to bolster their child's confidence through embracing the seven essential attributes. The reflections and actionable advice at the end of each chapter are especially valuable for parents looking for more tools to support their children. This book is for anyone preparing for parenthood or seeking to enhance their parenting skills!"

–Suzanne Morgan, retired teacher

"Brian Butler's book is a consistent source of optimism about America's kids despite his intimate understanding of the current imperfect educational system and the children who fall through its cracks. Butler takes a hopeful and encouraging viewpoint and clearly identifies solutions and actions parents and educators can take as a team today to help develop our future geniuses. Reading this book is a heartening experience and demonstrates clearly for parents their role in building their child's complete life experience."

–Lisa Wolfe and Byron Schrecker, parents of three children who attended Butler's Mason Crest Elementary School

"*Limitless Future* stands out for its clarity and practicality in guiding parents through the development of key attributes that pave the way for a limitless future for their children. This book's engaging examples and insightful reflections will help parents foster their child's growth and mentor their child on their journey to a fulfilling and successful life."

–Nikki Heinlein, retired teacher

"As a parent and an educator of 20+ years, this book empowers parents to be that rock for their child and spoke to my heart! Brian Butler educates parents about the parts of the brain, what happens in each area, and *why*. Knowing this is very important to developing their child's seven essential attributes. Intertwining his life experiences, humor, and other passionate people's stories, Brian provides reflection questions for parents, examples of how parents can talk with their child to develop these key attributes, and opportunities to help their child truly find their own inner voice, confidence, and passion!"

–Karen Olweiler, mother of two children and educator

"I am thrilled to endorse *Limitless Future*, a transformative work by Brian Butler. As I delved into the pages, I was transported back to my early years growing up in Salisbury, Maryland, where Brian and I were both raised. My fond memories of playing basketball in his backyard and knowing his family only add to my admiration for this latest endeavor. I am profoundly impressed by this book's ability to provide parents with a clear roadmap to success.

Brian is an esteemed educator who has truly walked in the footsteps of those who have shaped our educational landscape. This book is an essential read and deserves a place in the hands of every parent and others who want an unlimited future for the children they know!"

–Floyd Wilson, M.S. Ed, Dean of Students,
Kansas City, Missouri School District

LIMITLESS
FUTURE

LIMITLESS FUTURE

An Action Guide to Nurturing
Your Child's Unique Strengths,
Passions, and Talents

Brian Butler

Published by The Answer's In The Room Press

THE ANSWER'S IN
THE ROOM PRESS

To contact the author about speaking, workshops, or bulk orders of this book, visit https://www.brianbutler.info

ISBN (paperback): 979-8-9888579-2-1
ISBN (ebook): 979-8-9888579-3-8

Editor: David Aretha
Book design: Christy Day, Constellation Book Services
Book consultant and coach: Martha Bullen, Bullen Publishing Services

Library of Congress Control Number: 2024917948

Printed in the United States of America

Dedication

To my parents, Paul and Doris Butler,
my first and most important teachers

Without my parents, I would not be the person I am today. First and foremost, they taught me the values of kindness, humility, and respect for everyone. Observing their grace, humility, and compassion toward others taught me to love people, all people, and help when I could without expecting anything in return. They allowed me to work on a farm near my town throughout high school, where my main job was shoveling manure in massive chicken houses. This instilled in me the belief that no job or profession was beneath me and that there is honor and value in all work. At the same time, they wanted to impart the message that if I wanted to do other things in life, I would need to continue learning and growing. Most importantly, although they grew up in times of segregation, they modeled and taught me that bitterness and victimhood were unbecoming attitudes and would not serve me well; in fact, bitterness and victimhood would hold me back from having a positive and productive life.

In my early childhood, I struggled with learning to read, particularly decoding words and reading fluidly. In early elementary school, my teacher suggested to my parents that I be retained. My parents refused to accept this recommendation. My dad, a reading teacher, provided the necessary support at home, ensuring I eventually caught up. From what we know today about the effects of retention from esteemed researcher John Hattie, retaining a child severely negatively impacts their life, no matter how well-intentioned educators may be.

Since I mentioned John Hattie, let me take a side trip to support the notion that retention or holding a student back is a practice we should not be holding onto in the twenty-first century. John Hattie's research doesn't involve just a few studies. It's the most comprehensive and extensive research in the history of education. His latest dataset synthesizes 1,500 meta-analyses of 90,000 studies involving more than 300 million students. This is the world's most extensive evidence of what practices will most likely improve student learning.

In the International Media Center interview, Hattie said, *"No single intervention by schools is worse than retention. The major reason why retention is so harmful is that the child is subjected to the SAME curricula, often the SAME assignments, and often the SAME form of teaching. What this child needs is DIFFERENT teaching—the first time did not work. It also sets a clear expectation of failure. There can be many other reasons, but the fundamental effect is negative—just do not do it."*[1]

My parents were ahead of their time in understanding this. I can't imagine what my life would have been like or where I would be if my parents had allowed that well-meaning teacher to retain me. My early teacher did not know better. We know better today!

Beyond academics, my parents enriched my life with diverse experiences and opportunities. They introduced me to sports like basketball, football, and tennis and broadened my horizons through travel, taking us to theater, exposing us to opera, and providing numerous other social interactions. Their sacrifices, such as waking up early, driving us to practices and games, and volunteering to support our participation, made me realize how important they were to my success. When I was the age of eight in 1973, my parents took me, my brother Paul, and my sister Monica to see the Jackson 5. Although school is important, you can't put a price on or replicate these types of learning experiences. These experiences helped me develop the essential character skills/attributes discussed in this book, which are crucial for success.

---

1 John Hattie, "No single intervention by schools is worse than retention," Communications Unlimited, https://www.communications-unlimited.nl/no-single-intervention-by-schools-is-worse-than-retention/, accessed May 5, 2024.

These attributes guided me through grade school, high school, and college, and they continued to benefit me as a Division I athlete, a professional athlete, and an educator. These skills require constant reflection and improvement, but they have been invaluable throughout my life and career.

My parents' dedication, from reading to my siblings and me to engaging in meaningful conversations at the dinner table to providing a host of healthy hobbies, cultivated the 7 Essential Attributes I will explore in this book: **persistence**, **precise communication**, **self-control**, **empathy**, **curiosity**, **flexible thinking**, and **optimism**. Without my parents modeling and reinforcing these skills, I wouldn't be where I am today. Although my school experiences were generally positive, they were often inconsistent, teacher to teacher, year to year.

As a parent of two adult children and an educator for over thirty-five years, I've realized that to provide your child with a limitless future, you must continually provide opportunities and experiences necessary for your child to learn these essential attributes (behaviors/skills/attitudes).

This book is dedicated to my parents, the late Paul Butler Sr. and my mom, Doris Butler, because this version of Brian Butler would not exist today without them.

I hope this book elevates you as a parent so you can create a Limitless Future with your child.

–Brian Butler

Contents

Notes to Readers

In writing *Limitless Future: An Action Guide to Nurturing Your Child's Unique Strengths, Passions, and Talents,* I was reminded of a former student, Kaiulani Kimbrell, an actress, songwriter, singer, and single parent. Kaiulani's journey and creative process behind her album, which features the song "Limitless," resonate deeply with the themes of this book. Kaiulani's reflection on the genesis of her work encapsulates the essence of embracing growth and transformation.

"I wrote 'Limitless' in Mumbai, India. I went there in 2016 and started writing that album around then. I remember sitting by the Ganga River in northern India. The vibration of that river is so high, so holy, so beautiful, and so sacred. With everything I had gone through in my life, I wanted to create a body of work that elevated you."
—Kaiulani Kimbrell, singer/songwriter, actress, writer, activist, and producer[2]

Boorish Redundancy

One of my mentors and dear friends, the late Rick DuFour, used to say that if you want to communicate an idea or concept crystal clearly, you must express it repeatedly with "boorish redundancy." Throughout the book, certain ideas, concepts, or terms may be reiterated, revisited, or presented slightly differently to ensure clear understanding. My experience has shown that upon initially encountering an idea, clarity might not immediately ensue. Still, upon revisiting it after further reading or different experiences, I often perceive it in a new light. As author Brené Brown suggests, clear is

---

2 Kaiulani Kimbrel, personal communication, July 22, 2024.

kind, and unclear is unkind[3]; therefore, in the spirit of kindness, certain parts of the book may appear redundantly expressed, albeit from a slightly different perspective.

Parents

Please be aware that whenever the term *parent* appears in this book, it encompasses anyone directly involved and responsible for raising a child, including biological parents, stepparents, grandparents, aunts, uncles, adoptive parents, single parents, foster parents, those in blended family homes, and anyone legally responsible for raising a child.

---

3 Brené Brown, "Clear is Kind. Unclear is Unkind.," BreneBrown.com, October 15, 2018, https://brenebrown.com/articles/2018/10/15/clear-is-kind-unclear-is-unkind/, accessed May 24, 2024.

About This Book

Understanding how to do something is essential, but the why sets the stage for true change and learning. Often, the most significant error in change and learning is focusing solely on what and how while neglecting the deeper purpose. For parents, embracing new beliefs about learning, the brain, and the growth mindset requires a willingness to confront their adult and childhood experiences, biases, questions, and concerns. This willingness is crucial for true growth and transformation.

Chapter 1 lays the foundation by sharing the research, reasoning, and rationale behind the belief that our children have a limitless future. It encourages parents to be reflective and open to new insights grounded in the latest research and common sense about learning. Think of Chapter 1 as the soil and Chapters 2 through 8 (The 7 Essential Attributes That Foster Confidence in Our Children) as the seeds. Just as seeds need nutrient-rich soil to grow and flourish, Chapters 2 through 8 attributes will only take root and flourish if planted in the fertile ground of a well-prepared mind.

To truly embrace and implement the 7 Essential Attributes, parents must first believe in the richness of that soil—their beliefs. This means looking in the mirror and dispelling myths, long-held beliefs, and habits that limit what we think our children can achieve.

Finally, Chapter 9: Hopes and Dreams is akin to watching a fully grown plant, flower, or tree blossom. In this chapter, parents share their stories with the reader, including their hopes and dreams for their children.

CHAPTER 1

Foundations of Genius

"Many people die with their music still in them."
—Oliver Wendell Holmes[4]

Why Did I Write This Book?

As Gholdy Muhammad's insightful book *Cultivating Genius* (2020) suggests, there is genius in every one of your children, and it's our job as parents and as a society to help them believe this to be true so they can recognize their unique gifts.[5]

As I began writing this book, I had lunch with one of my education heroes and mentors, Lillie Jessie. During our conversation about my previous book, *Every Student Deserves a Gifted Education*, I expressed my deep passion for ensuring every child can live a life filled with endless possibilities, as my good friend Mike Mattos often says. Lillie then shared a profound insight from a relative, saying, *"Brian, so many people die with their song still in them."* At that moment, I realized that my purpose as an educator had never been so perfectly articulated. My mission has always been to help each child discover and share their "song" with the world!

4 Oliver Wendell Homes, "Quote," Goodreads, https://shorturl.at/KBOHO, accessed May 25, 2024.
5 Gholdy Muhammad, *Cultivating Genius*, Scholastic, 2020.

"While we wait for educational laws and mandates to embrace justice and equity, we must continue giving young people what they need to thrive in this world."
—Dr. Gholdy Muhammad[6]

Let me be candid. This book aims to empower *all* parents with straightforward, practical, and doable strategies, ideas, and resources to support their child's growth and development from birth to age eighteen.

I understand the immense challenges many parents face, especially those traditionally marginalized, from fully participating equally in our society. While various organizations and efforts address these societal inequities, this book encourages all parents to introspect and recognize their immense power in shaping their child's future regardless of family structure, ethnicity, zip code, culture, religion, or economic situation.

"The most common way people give up their power is by thinking they don't have any."
—Alice Walker[7]

I urge parents to confront a fundamental question and ask themselves: **What other choice do I have?** Parents possess the power to take immediate action within their sphere of influence. **Your child can't wait!**

This book encourages parents to reflect on their role in providing their children with essential experiences and opportunities to pursue their dreams. It's about taking proactive steps, leveraging the available resources, and fully preparing their child for an unlimited future of possibilities.

---

6 Gholdy Muhammad, "While we wait for…," Instagram post, accessed June 20, 2024.
7 Alice Walker, "Most Common Way People Give Up Their Power," 123HelpMe, https://www.123helpme.com/essay/Most-Common-Way-People-Give-Up-Their-F40752F57A98BCC4#google_vignette, accessed May 15, 2024.

By embracing this perspective, parents can positively influence their child's story, irrespective of external circumstances. Again, I am not in any way minimizing those external challenges. Some people may have a more challenging road ahead. But they must still travel that road or find a different one to reach their destination. This book guides parents seeking to make a tangible difference in their child's life today and for the rest of their lives by providing the mindset and skills that will give them the confidence to be successful.

"Give light, and people will find the way."
—Ella Baker[8]

As I began writing this book, I reflected on my parenting experience, which I shared with my wife, Kathleen. We had hopes and dreams for our daughters Alison and Emily's future. Our vision was that they would have a future where they could carve their paths and the resilience to overcome any obstacle, armed with the knowledge and skills they acquired while in our home.

Reflecting on Alison and Emily's lives from birth through adolescence, our goal was to help them become independent women when they eventually left our house. Kathleen's example of perseverance and independence set a powerful example for them. Their development was also greatly influenced by the diverse opportunities and experiences we provided them.

From an early age, Alison showed remarkable persistence and empathy, while Emily demonstrated kindness and an unwavering determination to excel. We also understood that their demonstrated qualities were not solely due to innate talent, skills, or character traits. It also reflected the values and principles that Kathleen and I had

8 Ella Baker, "Give light, and people will find the way," Pedagogy of Confidence, https://pedagogyofconfidence.net/, accessed May 24, 2024.

tried to teach and model, which were not always successful the first time. Whether it was Alison's artistic talent or Emily's commitment to mastering juggling a soccer ball, we made it a point to nurture their interests and passions by providing multiple opportunities and experiences.

As an educator for over three decades, a consultant who has traveled throughout the USA, Canada, and Australia, and one who led my last school as a principal with families who came from thirty-five birth countries and spoke over forty-two languages, I have interacted with countless parents, each sharing common hopes and dreams for their children. *It has been my experience that every parent sees their child as the apple of their eye and believes that the sky is the limit for their child.*

As parents, Kathleen and I made our fair share of mistakes, but with each misstep came a valuable lesson. If we could turn back time, armed with the knowledge we possess now, we would have approached some aspects of parenthood differently.

As you delve into the pages of this book, I invite you to reflect on your parenting and consider how you can celebrate each of your children's unique qualities. As you navigate the gift of parenting, the goal is for this book to assist you in equipping your children with the skills to believe that they have a limitless future to accomplish what they put their minds, body, and soul into.

All Children Start as Geniuses

In the book *The Genius in All of Us* (2010), David Shenk argues that individual differences in talent and intelligence are not solely determined by genes but develop over time through the dynamic interaction between genes and the environment.[9] While genetic differences play a significant role, they do not independently determine complex traits. Instead, this gene-environment interaction is a process we cannot

9 David Shenk, *The Genius in All of Us: New Insights into Genetics, Talents, and IQ*, Anchor Books, 2010.

fully control but can significantly influence... Broadly, limitations in achievement are not due to inadequate genetic assets but rather to our failure to tap into our existing capabilities.

In the 1960s, NASA initiated a groundbreaking study by Dr. George Land and his team to understand what makes a genius. Their objective was to identify the key characteristics that define exceptional problem-solving abilities. This endeavor commenced with a cohort of five-year-old participants who underwent a creativity test to assess their imaginative thinking and innovation capacity.

The astonishing results: 98 percent of the five-year-olds demonstrated genius in generating novel solutions and ideas. This initial revelation sparked intrigue and prompted further investigation into the developmental trajectory of creative aptitude.

Subsequent follow-ups at ages ten and fifteen revealed a concerning decline in creative thinking. By age ten, only 30 percent of the participants retained their "genius" status, and by age fifteen this figure plummeted to a mere 12 percent. This downward trend raised significant questions about the factors influencing the diminishing creativity observed in individuals as they progressed through adolescence.

Despite facing challenges and obstacles, Dr. Land's dedication to understanding the essence of creativity persisted. Broadening the scope of their study, the research team expanded their inquiries to include adults. The results were striking: only 2 percent of adults displayed traits suggesting creative genius.

"Oswald Spengler once said, after years of studying history, that it only takes 2% of the population to create the basic ideas, which the rest then apply. It turns out he was pretty close to right. If we're to face the future with hope, we can't rely on that anymore. What we found with those children is you have the potential to be part of that 98% genius."
—Dr. George Land

The above revelation underscored the profound impact of societal and educational influences on developing and expressing creative genius. Dr. Land attributed this decline in creative capacity primarily to the constraints imposed by traditional educational systems, which often prioritize standardized testing and conformity over divergent thinking and innovation.

In explaining how creativity works, Dr. Land delved into the different types of thinking that our brains engage in. He described *divergent thinking*, where we brainstorm many ideas, and *convergent thinking*, where we evaluate those ideas to select the best one. He emphasized how our education often focuses too much on convergent thinking, which can stifle our natural creativity.

Ultimately, Dr. Land's message was clear: we need to rethink how we approach education, tap into our inner "five-year-olds," and unleash our imagination to tackle the challenges of tomorrow.[10]

The First Architects: Parents' Crucial Role in Early Brain Development

For parents with children under three, let me speak directly to you for just a moment. Dana Suskind's insights emphasize your pivotal role in your children's brain development during the first three years of life. This period is critical as a significant portion of brain growth is completed by age four. The early language environment profoundly impacts a child's future cognitive and emotional capabilities.

Suskind explains that the quantity and quality of words children hear stimulate essential brain regions responsible for grammar, meaning, and emotional regulation. A rich verbal environment lays a strong foundation for later learning and behavior.

---

10 George Land, "The Failure Of Success." TEDxTucson, YouTube, December 2011, https://www.youtube.com/watch?v=ZfKMq-rYtnc&t=15s, accessed May 25, 2024.

Suskind's books, *Parent Nation* (2022)[11] and *Thirty Million Words* (2015)[12], highlight the crucial importance of language exposure. Children deprived of adequate verbal interaction may struggle to unlock their unlimited intellectual potential, akin to physical stunting from lack of nutrition. Commands and restrictions can hurt a child's ability to learn the language. For example, constantly telling a child "no" or "don't do that" can be negative. On the other hand, a diverse vocabulary and frequent family conversations are very beneficial. Parents who engage less verbally with their children tend to have children who speak less, underscoring the long-term impact of early linguistic interaction on a child's development.

Embracing the Power of Opportunity: A Parent's Role

In his seminal work, *Outliers* (2008), Malcolm Gladwell profoundly reflects on the nature of success. He challenges the prevailing myths that attribute achievement solely to individual brilliance or fortuitous circumstances. Instead, Gladwell directs our attention to a critical yet often overlooked factor: **opportunity**.

Consider the story of Bill Gates, a name synonymous with entrepreneurial prowess and innovation. Many marvel at the prodigious talents of young Gates, but Gladwell offers a different perspective. He reminds us that Gates' journey to success was not solely a product of his genius but a convergence of opportunity and circumstance.

In 1968, because of his father's contacts and influence, Gates was granted access to a time-sharing computer terminal—a pivotal moment that shaped his future endeavors. Gladwell raises a thought-provoking question: What if this opportunity had been available to numerous other teenagers?[13]

---

11 Dana Suskind, *Parent Nation*, Penguin Random House, 2022.
12 Dana Suskind, *Thirty Million Words*, Penguin Random House, 2015.
13 Malcolm Gladwell, *Outliers*, Little, Brown and Company, 2008.

The implication is clear: Success is not solely a matter of innate ability; it is about the opportunities available to us. As a parent, I believe this realization is of deep importance.

We often entrust the lion's share of our children's education to schools, believing they hold the keys to success. Yet, Gladwell's insights urge us to expand our perspective. While education is undeniably important, our role as parents extends far beyond the classroom walls.

We are the architects of our children's opportunities—the stewards of their limitless future. Relying solely on the school system, which may or may not provide the opportunities that your child needs to spark their curiosity and pursue their interests, is not enough. Instead, we must actively seek out and create opportunities that will enrich their lives and broaden their horizons.

This means exposing them to diverse experiences, igniting their interest, fostering their passions, and instilling a thirst for knowledge and exploration. It means cultivating resilience in the face of adversity and teaching them to seize opportunities with courage and determination.

As we navigate the journey of parenthood, let us heed Gladwell's wisdom and embrace our role as *architects of opportunity*. In doing so, we not only shape our children's destinies but also pave the way for a world where every individual can thrive.

SHARING HER SONG WITH THE WORLD: FOSTERING RAINA'S MUSICAL OPPORTUNITIES IN A MILITARY FAMILY

I began with the quote: "Many people die with their music still in them," inspired by Lillie Jessie's story. This is the perfect time to share the story of Raina, one of my former students who was with us for only a few years due to her family's military life. I asked Raina's mom, Angela Samosorn, to share how they provided different opportunities for Raina despite frequent moves.

The following narrative is an excerpt from a questionnaire completed by Angela. It reflects her family's goal to provide Raina with as many opportunities and experiences as possible as a military family that moved several times. This is written in Angela's voice, although it has been adapted for length and style.

As a military family, our life with Raina has constantly changed. Our hopes centered around her happiness and ability to adjust to frequent moves. As she grew older, we realized factors beyond our control shaped her experiences.

As Raina has aged, especially since starting high school, I've consistently hoped she realizes her worth. I hope she feels her worth and value as an individual, a future educator, and a woman every day. As she finishes high school, we hope she finds happiness and fulfillment in whatever path she chooses.

Encouraging Raina to explore various activities has been crucial. Despite the challenges of being a military child, we said "yes" to her desires. We wanted Raina to discover what brought her joy, from museums to sports and music.

Music has been significant for her. From her early fascination with the violin in Italy to her love for the band in middle school, Raina's musical journey has brought her joy and growth. She embraced the saxophone and found community in the band. Moving to Texas, she continued her dedication, eventually becoming Drum Major, a role that filled her with pride.

Raina also explored other fine arts, from school musicals to tech theater. Each experience contributed to her growth. She is excited and determined as she approaches her final year of high school.

Reflecting on Raina's journey, I recall her decision to stop swimming—a significant part of her life. Her father reminded me that Raina needed to follow her path. It wasn't easy, but seeing her passion for music helped me understand that letting go can be best for our children.

Over the years, we've learned to step back and become guides rather than directors in her life. Despite challenges, seeing her pursue her dreams has been rewarding. As she embarks on the next chapter, we are grateful for her opportunities and the person she has become. Our love and support for her remain constant, no matter where her journey takes her. She is well-equipped to face challenges, driven by her passion.

In Angela's story about Raina, the theme of access, opportunities, and experiences stands out. These experiences revealed Raina's genius. Everyone has genius within them, and each child starts as a genius.[14]

Looking for Immediate Help in the Wrong Place

"Your whole life, sir, you have followed the wrong star."
—Blind Man Cassidy[15]

In Dana Suskind's book *Parent Nation* (2022), she writes about the concept of the streetlight effect.[16] We often gravitate toward easily accessible solutions, even if they aren't the most effective. By fixating solely on K-12 education, we overlook the critical early years when a child's mind is most receptive to growth and development, as well as throughout their schooling when we, their parents—their first teachers—have a responsibility to work with, support, and make the local school the best it can be. Simultaneously, you are responsible for preparing your child to face the challenges they will encounter in school and life by providing opportunities and experiences outside and

---

14 Angela Samosorn, personal memo, June 9, 2024.
15 *Red Dead Redemption II* (video game).
16 Dana Suskind, *Parent Nation*, 2022, Penguin Random House, p. 51

inside of school that will nurture their unique strengths, passions, and talents—their gifts!

It's time to realign our focus. We must acknowledge that our children's success should not be solely reliant on the school they attend. As parents, we are responsible for providing the tools and resources necessary for our children's growth and development.

If you are looking for our traditional school system to be the savior of your child, you are looking in the wrong place. Throughout my career as an educator, I have worked alongside and observed educators who are excellent at what they do. Great, hard-working people who care deeply about their students. Yet, like placing water in an ice tray that will freeze and form into ice cubes overnight, many educators will conform to our traditional system, which is not designed to nurture each child's unique strengths, passions, and talents. And it's not the fault of an individual educator! The Traditional System is slow to change and constantly at the whim of policymakers, political forces, and, to be honest, initiative fatigue from many school systems.

Initiative fatigue occurs almost yearly when many new ideas or initiatives promise to be the magic pill for education. Still, for whatever reason—leadership changes, lack of persistence with the initiative, educators not having the training to implement what they are asked to, and lack of understanding of the reasons behind implementing a new initiative—these attempts often lead to a lack of success, and the cycle repeats.

Suppose you are a parent who is also an educator interested in genuinely reimagining traditional gifted education. In that case, I highly recommend my companion book for educators, *Every Student Deserves a Gifted Education: 5 Shifts to Nurturing Each Student's Unique Strengths, Passions, and Talents* (2023).[17]

---

17 Brian Butler, *Every Student Deserves a Gifted Education*, The Answer's In The Room Press, 2023.

"There's wonderful work happening in this country, but I have to say it's happening in spite of the dominant culture of education, not because of it. It's like people are sailing into a headwind all the time."
—Ken Robinson[18]

While some schools and districts have embraced effective models that focus on a collaborative approach in which all stakeholders take collective responsibility for each child in the school, an approach of vulnerability and sharing practices around specific questions to ensure all students have systematic support, there remains a disparity in educational approaches nationwide and, in turn, outcomes. My book *Every Student Deserves a Gifted Education* aims to reimagine the system from gifted education for the select few to gifted education for all. I provided a roadmap for schools and districts to reimagine and change today's traditional gifted education. I highlighted inspirational school districts that *walk the talk* that every student should have access to gifted experiences. They are shining examples of what can be achieved when educators collaborate effectively. However, many schools continue to have teachers work in isolation or continue to create the illusion of a collaborative culture, often leaving teachers to fend for themselves. This hinders our goal of nurturing each student's unique strengths, passions, and talents.

In the appendix, I will provide some direct questions you can ask your school to determine whether it embraces an effective collaborative culture and what it is doing to provide a gifted experience to all children, regardless of their background.

We cannot and should not put all our faith in a traditional education system that was never designed for all students to succeed and is extremely slow to embrace systemic change. Instead, we must empower ourselves to actively support our children's learning from infancy to

---

18 Ken Robinson, "How to escape education's Death Valley," TED, YouTube, May 10, 2023. https://www.youtube.com/watch?v=wX78iKhInsc, accessed May 25, 2024.

adolescence. By doing so, we ensure they have every opportunity to thrive in any situation they might find themselves in.

How Understanding Brain Development Can Help Parents Support Their Child's Learning

Teaching Toward Genius
—Dr. Yvette Jackson

Yvette Jackson: "Kids have enormous potential, and when we…act like they're gifted, they will show us their gifts; in fact, they will surpass them. We should always be teaching towards genius!"

Yolanda Sealy-Ruiz: "But we should remember that we start out as geniuses."

Yvette Jackson: "That's right."

Yolanda Sealy-Ruiz: "This is not new for us!"[19]

As parents, it's essential to recognize the ever-changing world of education and the critical role of understanding the science of learning and the brain in nurturing our children's limitless potential. Throughout my career as an educator, spanning over thirty-five years, I've observed a significant gap in educators' understanding of these fundamental concepts. In my previous book, *Every Student Deserves a Gifted Education*, I dedicated a section of the first chapter to clarifying the brain's workings and its impact on learning for educators.

However, as educators may find themselves navigating this new learning, so too might parents. In *this book*, I aim to bridge this gap by providing parents with foundational knowledge about the science of learning. By demystifying these concepts and presenting them in

---

19 Yvette Jackson and Yolanda Sealy-Ruiz, conversation exchange, Facebook Live webinar, February 8, 2020.

accessible language, we can ensure that all parents have a level playing field when supporting their children.

This section on the brain is intended to provide basic information. It is not meant to be an in-depth exploration of neuroscience.

As children grow, their brains continually change in response to their experiences, whether it's a playdate with a friend or hearing a favorite bedtime story. These early interactions help refine the brain's circuits for seeing, hearing, feeling, and acting in the world. When children start school, they need to adapt these brain circuits in new ways to learn how to read, write, and understand math. Scientists and educators are collaborating to study these changes to improve learning processes.

In the article "Putting Neuroscience in the Classroom: How the Brain Changes As We Learn" (2020), Bruce McCandliss and Elizabeth Toomarian wrote about Synapse School in Menlo Park, California, Stanford University (2020), where neuroscientists work closely with teachers to observe how children's brains develop.[20] Students visit the Brainwave Learning Center, wearing caps with sensors that measure brain waves while playing educational games or practicing mindfulness. This hands-on experience allows children to see their brain activity and understand how learning and mindset shifts affect their brains. This knowledge can empower children to take ownership of their learning.

This research combines the fields of neuroscience and education, providing valuable insights into how different learning experiences influence brain development. For instance, understanding how classroom learning impacts brain circuits can help explain why some children struggle with learning and how education can be tailored to support them better.

---

20 Bruce McCandliss and Elizabeth Toomarian, "Putting Neuroscience in the Classroom: How the Brain Changes As We Learn," Pew, April 13, 2020, https://www.pewtrusts.org/en/trend/archive/spring-2020/putting-neuroscience-in-the-classroom-how-the-brain-changes-as-we-learn, accessed May 28, 2024.

One notable example is a large-scale brain development study involving 11,000 third graders nationwide who undergo brain scans every two years. This study explores the diversity of brain development and its connection to education, including how different environments and activities influence brain and skill development.

Understanding that learning experiences physically change their child's brain can be incredibly powerful for parents. It highlights the importance of providing enriching, supportive environments at home. By recognizing the significance of these experiences, parents can better support their child's educational journey, from encouraging reading and math skills to fostering creativity and emotional growth.

When children understand how their brains change with learning, they can approach learning opportunities and experiences inside and outside school with curiosity and empowerment. This growing field of educational neuroscience offers exciting possibilities for improving educational practices and helping all children unleash their limitless potential.

"My 5-year-old explained to me that it's OK when she makes a mistake because she's growing the neurons in her brain. I just want to hug her teacher."
—Erin Brisbin[21]

What Are Neurons?

Our brains are incredible, containing around 85 billion tiny nerve cells called neurons. Neurons are essential for thinking, moving, and feeling. Picture a neuron like a tree: the branches are called dendrites, which catch signals from other neurons. These signals are special chemicals called neurotransmitters.

---

21 "Edutopia," Instagram, https://www.instagram.com/edutopia/, accessed May 29, 2024.

The signals travel to the main part of the neuron, the soma. If the signal is strong enough, it moves down a long part called the axon, similar to a highway for the signal. At the end of the axon, the signal triggers the release of neurotransmitters, which then travel to the next neuron's dendrites, continuing the process. This is how neurons communicate and make our brains work.

The Brain Regions/Parts

Cerebrum: The largest part of the brain, responsible for learning and thinking. It has two halves called hemispheres, connected by the corpus callosum, which allows them to communicate. The cerebrum's wrinkled outer layer, the cerebral cortex, handles many higher mental functions.

Prefrontal Cortex: Located in the front of the cerebrum, behind the forehead. It's key for decision-making, problem-solving, and logical thinking. It helps us plan, control emotions, set goals, and shape our personality and values.

Amygdala: A small structure deep within the cerebrum, acting as the brain's emotional center. It processes emotions like happiness, fear, anger, and excitement and is crucial in recognizing and responding to emotional situations.

Hippocampus: Found deep in the cerebrum, close to the center. It's vital for forming and retrieving memories, helping us store and remember information, events, and experiences. It's essential for learning new things and recalling memories.

Cerebellum: Located below the cerebrum at the back of the brain, often called the "Little Brain." It involves coordination, balance, and precise movements, helping with walking, running, writing, and playing sports.

Brain Stem: Connects directly to the spinal cord at the base of the brain, below the cerebellum. It controls essential functions like breathing, heart rate, blood pressure, digestion, and sleep, regulating many vital bodily tasks without conscious thought.

Image 1.1

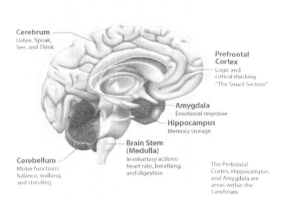

OUR BRAIN
The Cerebrum, Cerebellum, and Brain Stem

Why Is It Important for Parents to Understand the Brain?

Understanding the brain and its parts helps parents support their children's learning and development. Here's why it's important and what parents can do:

1. Early Brain Development: Parents play a key role in early brain development, especially in the first three years. Talking, reading, and conversing stimulate brain regions responsible for language, cognition, and emotional regulation.

Dana Suskind's insights emphasize your pivotal role in your children's brain development during the first three years of life. This period is critical as a significant portion of brain growth is completed by age four. The early language environment profoundly impacts a child's future cognitive and emotional capabilities.

2. Neuroplasticity: Children's brains are adaptable and grow in response to experiences. Creating enriching environments with diverse experiences and problem-solving activities fosters learning and development.

3. Brain Regions and Functions: Knowing brain regions and their functions helps parents understand their children's behaviors and emotions. For example, the prefrontal cortex, responsible for decision-making, develops significantly during adolescence. Supporting this with problem-solving skills and emotional intelligence is beneficial.

4. Memory Formation and Learning: The hippocampus is crucial for memory and learning. Parents can help by providing opportunities for repetition, active learning, and meaningful experiences, enhancing memory retention and cognitive processing.

5. Motor Skills and Coordination: The cerebellum is essential for developing physical activities and motor skills. Activities promoting balance, coordination, and fine motor skills, like sports and arts, support this development.

In exploring brain development and its impact on parenting, meraki. motherhood presents a compelling perspective emphasizing the crucial link between understanding how children's brains function, learn, and grow and making informed decisions as parents. It stresses the significance of fostering play-based learning environments for young children. The excerpt reminds parents to advocate for learning environments that support their children's natural inclination for exploration and movement, facilitating optimal brain development and learning outcomes.[22]

---

22 "meraki.motherhood," Instagram reel, https://www.instagram.com/reel/C7SrB8mphY-/?igsh=MWk2azltOWphcnV6Zg%3D%3D.

Gabor Maté stresses that play is crucial for healthy brain development. Adults (parents and schools) should focus on creating conditions supporting brain development by fostering nurturing relationships, providing ample play opportunities, and encouraging interaction and spontaneity. Such an environment nurtures children's natural curiosity and creativity, allowing them to learn naturally.[23]

6. Emotional Regulation and Well-being: The amygdala processes emotions. Parents can help children develop emotional intelligence and resilience by modeling healthy coping strategies and teaching social awareness, self-awareness, and self-regulation.

Brain Chemicals—Neurotransmitters[24]

Cortisol—The Stress Chemical:

Cortisol helps manage bodily functions and stress. However, chronic stress can lead to prolonged high cortisol levels, causing issues like high blood pressure, anxiety, depression, memory problems, and sleep troubles. Children under constant stress are particularly vulnerable, as prolonged stress impacts learning abilities.

Happiness Chemicals:

Four main chemicals regulate happiness in the brain:

1. **Dopamine:** Fuels motivation, learning, and pleasure.

2. **Oxytocin:** Builds trust and sustains relationships, known as the "Cuddle or Love Hormone."

3. **Serotonin:** Enhances feelings of significance and self-acceptance, promoting calmness and confidence.

---

23 Andre Duqum, "Insightful episode from @knowthyself podcast episode 33 with @gabormatemd," Instagram, @parenting_my_teen.
24 Adapted from *Every Student Deserves a Gifted Education*, 2023.

4. **Endorphins:** Act as natural painkillers, offering euphoria and alleviating anxiety and depression.

Deficiencies in Happiness Chemicals

Dopamine: Leads to procrastination, low self-esteem, lack of motivation, fatigue, and anxiety.

Oxytocin: Causes loneliness, stress, disconnection, and insomnia.

Serotonin: Results in low self-esteem, mood swings, anxiety disorders, and depression.

Endorphins: Leads to anxiety, depression, body aches, mood swings, and impulsive behaviors.

Boosting Happiness Chemicals

Dopamine: Meditation, achievable goals, L-Tyrosine-rich foods (avocados, eggs), enjoyable exercise, and creative activities.

Oxytocin: Physical touch, social interactions, petting pets, massages, acupuncture, music, exercise, and cold showers.

Serotonin: Regular exercise, sunlight, serotonin-boosting foods (bananas, omega-3 fish), massage therapy, and cold showers.

Endorphins: Laughter, creative expression, dark chocolate, spicy foods, exercise, high-intensity training, massage therapy, and meditation.

Why Is It Important for Parents to Understand Brain Chemicals?

Understanding brain chemicals impacts children's physical, emotional, and mental well-being:

1. **Managing Stress and Health:** Recognizing prolonged stress helps parents identify stress signs and prevent related health issues.

2. **Fostering Emotional Well-being:** Knowledge of happiness chemicals helps create environments that enhance emotional health.

3. **Identifying and Addressing Deficiencies:** Parents can recognize and address neurotransmitter deficiencies, which support emotional balance. Consider consulting with a health professional if you have concerns about these areas.

4. **Promoting Healthy Lifestyle Choices:** Understanding the impact of these chemicals guides better lifestyle choices, like regular exercise, balanced nutrition, and positive social interactions.

5. **Enhancing Overall Development:** Better emotional regulation, improved academic performance, stronger social skills, and greater resilience.

By understanding neurotransmitters, parents can support their children's health and happiness, leading to balanced and fulfilling lives.

"Change the input, and the brain changes accordingly."
—Reuven Feuerstein[25]

This book is designed to empower all parents with practical strategies to support their child's growth and development every moment from birth to age eighteen. Our goal should be to provide our children with many opportunities and experiences for enjoyment, interaction,

---

25 "The Pedagogy of Confidence," Eggplant, https://eggplant.org/the-pedagogy-of-confidence-2, accessed June 1, 2024.

and exploration across various avenues, allowing them to discover their interests and strengths.

If your child has an interest, even if you don't see the value of the interest in something that can help them have a better life as an adult, please support them in pursuing it. Anytime your child has an interest and a passion for something, and they can't stop thinking about it, or it excites them when they participate in it, whether it's gardening or playing a musical instrument, they are learning skills like persistence, self-control, etc. They are developing new skills, and as they grow, they can transfer the skill set they've learned from their childhood passions and pursuits to things they need as they're growing up. We should also give kids various sampling experiences to see what gives them joy. Maybe it wasn't soccer, but they got excited when they joined the robotics club. Perhaps it wasn't drawing, but learning to cook new recipes motivated them.

Recognizing that children are dynamic beings with evolving interests and capabilities is essential. What may initially seem like a natural inclination or ease may not define them entirely, and initial challenges can transform into strengths through perseverance and focused practice. Therefore, we must avoid rigidly labeling children based on early interests, ensuring they have the freedom to explore and grow in various directions.

In his book *Hidden Potential* (2023), Adam Grant urges us not to pigeonhole individuals into rigid learning styles. While preferences exist, they are not fixed, and focusing solely on strengths can impede growth. Actual growth often arises from embracing discomfort, stepping outside our comfort zones, and confronting challenges head-on. As Grant underscores, "true courage lies in discarding the safety of our comfort zones and embracing the vast realm of possibility."[26]

---

26 Adam Grant, *Hidden Potential*, Viking Press, 2023.

Cultivating a Growth Mindset and Overcoming Fear Mindset

A learner...
Believes that anyone can change their
current intelligence and abilities.
Believes that learning is a skill.
Believes that learning is in their control.
Understands that mistakes, obstacles, setbacks, and struggles are a
normal and necessary part of learning and expects them to happen.
Acknowledges effort and discomfort as a
normal and necessary part of growth.
Makes the choice to frame challenges into opportunities to grow
instead of reasons to get frustrated, give up, or deflect.
Leans into the discomfort that may arise, focusing on the
process and the incremental growth that results.[27]

One of the most empowering realizations for children and parents is understanding that intelligence and talent are not fixed traits but malleable qualities that can be cultivated and nurtured. By embracing challenges, fostering curiosity, cultivating persistence, viewing effort as a pathway to mastery, and learning from feedback and others, children can unlock their limitless potential.

Chapter 8 of David Shenk's book *The Genius in All of Us* (2010) challenges the notion of fixed intelligence and inherent abilities, advocating instead for a view of human potential as malleable and shaped by genetic predispositions and environmental influences. According to Shenk, behaviors like intelligence, athletic prowess, and creativity are not predetermined but are outcomes of ongoing developmental processes.[28]

---

27 Mineolagrows.com, accessed June 1, 2024.
28 David Shenk, *The Genius in All of Us*, Anchor Books, 2010.

Andrew Meltzoff, a researcher at the University of Washington, underscores that children are not born intelligent but are designed to learn and adapt based on their experiences. This perspective rejects the idea of fixed abilities, emphasizing instead the importance of nurturing and engaging with a child's evolving capabilities from early on.

Parents are encouraged to recognize and respect the dynamic nature of their child's development, understanding that their unique personality begins to form even before birth. Like how researchers observe interactions between genetics and environment in scientific studies, parents witness firsthand how their child's biology interacts with the world around them, shaping preferences, emotions, and abilities.

Ultimately, Shenk suggests that parents play a crucial role in providing genetic material and nurturing and guiding their child's growth. By embracing the inseparability of nature and nurture, parents can optimize the developmental process, supporting their child's potential to achieve in various athletic, intellectual, or creative domains.

As parents, we want to see our children thrive and succeed. A growth mindset is one of the most powerful tools we can provide them. This mindset, championed by researchers like Carol Dweck (2006), emphasizes the belief that abilities and intelligence can be developed through dedication and effort.[29]

The Growth Mindset says, "I believe I can learn." Neuroscience and understanding neuroplasticity reinforce this by saying, "You can learn."

On the other hand, there's what Carol Dweck termed a "fixed mindset." This mindset suggests that abilities and intelligence are innate and unchangeable. Those with a fixed mindset may believe that their talents and abilities are predetermined, leading them to avoid challenges and give up easily in the face of setbacks.

---

29 Carol Dweck, *Mindset: The New Psychology of Success*, Ballantine, 2006.

"Courage is not the absence of fear—
it's inspiring others to move beyond it."
—One of Nelson Mandela's "8 Lessons of Leadership"
(as reported by Richard Stengel)[30]

Recent work by Carol Dweck and David Yeager, particularly in 2020, has delved deeper into understanding growth and fear mindsets.[31] Their research highlights how addressing both the concept of a growth mindset and the fear mindset is crucial for fostering resilience and adaptability in children. They emphasize that merely knowing about the growth mindset is not enough; addressing the fears and anxieties that may hold individuals back from embracing challenges and learning from setbacks is essential.

A Powerful Message About Fear and Extraordinary Treasures Hidden Within You

In her book *Big Magic*, Elizabeth Gilbert talks about how you can embrace fear and put it in its proper perspective. Here is an excerpt of Elizabeth Gilbert's reading from that bestselling book about the emotion of fear at a Barnes & Noble in Manhattan on October 29, 2015:

"I even have a welcoming speech prepared for fear, which I deliver right before embarking on any new project or big adventure, and it goes like this:

Dearest fear, creativity and I are about to go on a road trip. I understand you'll be joining us because you always do. I acknowledge that you believe you have an important job to do in my

30 https://www.leadershipnow.com/leadingblog/2008/07/mandela_his_8_lessons_of_leade.html, accessed on June 1, 2024.
31 D. S. Yeager and C. S. Dweck, "What can be learned from growth mindset controversies?" *American Psychologist*, vol. 75, no. 9, 2020, pp. 1269-1279, https://doi.org/10.1037/amp0000794, https://psycnet.apa.org/record/2020-99903-019.

life, and you take your job seriously. Apparently, your job is to induce complete panic in me whenever I'm about to do anything interesting. And may I say, you are superb at your job. So, by all means, keep doing your job if you feel you must. But I will also be doing my job on this road trip, which is to work hard and stay focused, and creativity will be doing its job, which is to remain stimulating and inspiring. There's plenty of room in the minivan for all of us, so make yourself at home. But understand this: Creativity and I are the only ones who will be making any decisions along the way. I recognize and respect that you're part of this family. I will never exclude you from our activities. But still, your suggestions will not be followed. You are allowed to have a seat; you're allowed to have a voice, but you are not allowed to have a vote. You don't get to touch the road maps; you're not allowed to suggest detours; you're not allowed to fiddle with the temperature, dude; you're not even allowed to choose the freaking snacks. But above all else, my dear old familiar friend, you are absolutely forbidden to drive. And then we head off together, me and creativity and fear, side by side by side, forever marching once more into the terrifying but marvelous terrain of the unknown outcome.

Why is this worth it? It isn't always comfortable or easy carrying your fear around with you on your great and ambitious road trips. I mean, but it's always worth it because if you can't learn to travel comfortably alongside your fear, then you will never be able to go anywhere interesting or do anything interesting. And that would be a pity because your life is short and rare and amazing and miraculous, and you want to do really interesting things and make really interesting things while you're still here. I know that's what you want for yourself because that's what

I want for myself too. That's what we all want. And you have **treasures hidden within you, extraordinary treasures**, and so do I, and so does everyone around us. And bringing forth those treasures to light takes work and faith and focus and courage and hours of devotion. And the clock is ticking, and the world is spinning, and we simply do not have time anymore to think so small."[32]

With the Right Mindset and Approach, Virtually Everyone Can Improve and Excel in Various Areas of Life

Michael Merzenich (2004), a pioneer of neuroplasticity in neuroscience, has conducted groundbreaking research highlighting the human brain's incredible potential. He explains that the brain is massively plastic, meaning it can change and adapt throughout our lives, regardless of age or ability.

Merzenich's research shows that virtually everyone can improve and excel in various areas of life with the right mindset and approach. He emphasizes that the brain's plasticity is its greatest asset, enabling individuals to grow and develop continuously. As he puts it, "absolutely everyone can be better at virtually everything."

Merzenich's insights remind us that our limitless potential for growth and improvement knows no bounds. Our children can overcome challenges, learn new skills, and achieve their goals with dedication, perseverance, and a growth mindset. By nurturing this mindset in our children, we empower them to embrace learning and face challenges with resilience.[33]

---

32 Elizabeth Gilbert, reading from *Big Magic* about the emotion of fear, Barnes & Noble, Manhattan, October 29, 2015, https://shorturl.at/rACLP.
33 Michael Merzenich, "Growing Evidence of Brain Plasticity," *TED*, February 2004, https://www.ted.com/talks/michael_merzenich_growing_evidence_of_brain_plas-ticity?language=en.

Here's how you can help instill and nurture a growth mindset in your child while addressing fears and challenges:

In the article "What is Growth Mindset—Introduction to Growth Mindset Teaching," the authors from Big Life Journal shared 5 Tips for Teaching a Growth Mindset:

1. Embrace a Growth Mindset for Yourself First: Adults must believe in a growth mindset before teaching it to children. I highly recommend Carol Dweck's book *Mindset*.[34]

2. Provide an Introduction for Your Child with Analogies: To help children understand, compare building pathways in the brain to building a bridge or walking through tall grass. Share the story of "Revisiting Stella," which you will read about in Chapter 2.

3. Introduce Mindset with Examples: Discuss tasks that were once difficult but became easier with practice to illustrate the benefits of persistence.

4. Emphasize the Learning Process: Focus on the learning process rather than the outcome.

5. Give Yourself and Your Children Grace: Understand and practice giving grace when mistakes are made for yourself and your children.[35]

A growth mindset encourages taking risks, learning from failures, and persevering. It fosters curiosity, resilience, and a love of learning, believing that abilities can be developed through dedication and effort. Encourage children to think about times when they've faced challenges and how they

---

34 Carol Dweck, *Mindset: The New Psychology of Success*, Ballantine, 2006.
35 "What is Growth Mindset—Introduction to Growth Mindset Teaching." *Big Life Journal*, https://shorturl.at/exruY and https://empoweringeducation.org/. The authors shared 5 Tips for Teaching a Growth Mindset.

overcame them. Ask them how they can apply a growth mindset to their everyday lives, whether in school, sports, hobbies, or friendships.

Encourage Effort: Celebrate your child's effort and perseverance instead of praising outcomes or natural talent. Highlight the value of hard work leading to growth and improvement.

Embrace Challenges: Encourage your child to take on challenges, seeing them as opportunities to learn and grow rather than threats to their abilities.

Normalize Mistakes: Teach your child that making mistakes is a natural part of learning and provides valuable feedback. Encourage them to learn from mistakes rather than fear them.

Address Fear Mindset: Acknowledge and address any fears or anxieties your child may have about failure or making mistakes. Help them understand that it's okay to feel afraid but important not to let fear hold them back from trying new things or pursuing their goals.

Value Learning: Foster a love of learning by emphasizing the joy and satisfaction of acquiring new skills and knowledge, viewing learning as a lifelong journey.

Model a Growth Mindset: Demonstrate a growth mindset by openly discussing your challenges and how you overcome them through effort and perseverance.

Provide Supportive Feedback: Offer feedback focused on specific efforts and strategies rather than innate abilities. Encourage your child to see feedback as a valuable tool for improvement.

Cultivate a Safe Environment: Create a safe and supportive environment where your child feels comfortable taking risks and making mistakes. Emphasize that failures are an essential part of learning and offer encouragement and support.

By fostering a growth mindset and addressing fears, you're equipping your child with the resilience, perseverance, and confidence they need to navigate life's challenges and tap into their limitless potential. Together, you can cultivate a mindset that values effort, embraces challenges, and celebrates the journey of learning and growth.

Mineola Grows, and Your Brain Does, Too!

Although the primary focus of this book centers on empowering parents with immediate strategies for fostering the growth and development of their children, I began the section about the concept of mindset with a quote from the website of an exceptional school district on Long Island, New York: Mineola School District. Regarded as a premier and forward-thinking school district whose work on growth mindset is unparalleled, it has developed a comprehensive online resource center dedicated to promoting a growth mindset among students. This invaluable resource includes informative videos and learner guides on brain function, neuron development, and emotional intelligence. Superintendent Michael Nagler and his team have generously made these resources available for free, extending their benefits to students, their families, and all individuals seeking to support children's education. Whether you're looking to assist your child, yourself, or your school, I highly recommend exploring this outstanding website—it's truly fantastic: https://www.mineolagrows.com/series/howmybrainworks

Failure: The True Path to Success

I have always been fascinated with Kareem Abdul-Jabbar. Not only was he a great basketball player, but he has dared to challenge us to be better versions of ourselves as human beings each day. Kareem writes an online newsletter, and this is his message about failure, starting with a quote from Michael Jordan:

Kareem's Daily Quote

"I've missed more than 9000 shots in my career. I've lost almost 300 games. Twenty-six times, I've been trusted to take the game-winning shot and missed. I've failed over and over and over again in my life. And that is why I succeed."
—Michael Jordan

For me, this quote means something different than what it appears to say. For most, Michael is extolling the necessity of failure in the formula for success. He's right. After so many failed experiments involving the light bulb, Thomas Edison was encouraged by others to quit, to which he responded, "I haven't failed—I've just found 10,000 ways that won't work." These quotes encourage us to keep trying, knowing that so many successful people experienced the same failures and disappointments. I'm on board with that interpretation.

But I also see another way to look at it that is equally inspiring. Instead of defining success as a level of achievement—winning the trophy, getting the promotion—I like to think of success as simply enjoying playing in the game. Failure to win is not failure. Those who never hoist a shiny trophy overhead or drive around in a Tesla haven't lost a thing; they are always in the process of winning because every day they step onto the court of their lives and just enjoy the game, the interaction with other players, the feel of the ball in their hands, the joy of movement. Every day they engage with humanity with good cheer, just happy to be in the game—and that is why they succeed. Success isn't winning but choosing to play and choosing to enjoy playing.[36]

This chapter focused on clarifying any misunderstandings or long-held myths about learning. To be clear, learning is a Universal Skill that we can continually improve.

We now will turn our attention to essential skills, behaviors, and attributes, which we will call attributes, which become paramount as our world evolves with technological advancements. In his book *Hidden Potential* (2023), Adam Grant states that while cognitive abilities set us apart from animals, our character skills distinguish us from machines.[37] As automation takes over cognitive tasks, we're witnessing a revolution where human qualities such as interactions and relationships are becoming increasingly crucial.

Now, we explore the *7 Essential Attributes that foster confidence in children.* These attributes, referred to by some as character strengths or traits, are fundamentally human skills that hold the key to unlocking our children's limitless potential in any avenue of learning they choose to pursue.

Fostering Confidence in Students
with 7 Essential Attributes

In the upcoming chapters, we'll delve into these 7 Essential Attributes:

Chapter 2: Fostering Persistence

Chapter 3: Nurturing Precise Communication

Chapter 4: Developing Self-control

---

36 Kareem Abdul-Jabbar, "Kareem's Daily Quote," Substack, July 5, 2024, kareem@ substack.com.
37 Adam Grant, *Hidden Potential*, Viking Press, p. 22.

Chapter 5: Building Empathy

Chapter 6: Encouraging Curiosity

Chapter 7: Embracing Flexible Thinking

Chapter 8: Cultivating Optimism

These attributes are the cornerstones upon which our children can construct a sturdy foundation for lifelong learning, growth, and fulfillment.

Consider the following scenario:

Imagine a child embarks on a project to build a model airplane. At first, they encounter difficulties following the instructions precisely, but their **persistence** drives them to keep trying until they get it right. Along the way they face setbacks, but their **optimism** fuels their belief that they can overcome any challenge.

As they work on the project, **precise communication** becomes essential when seeking help or clarifying instructions. Through clear communication, they express their ideas effectively and collaborate with others. This fosters **empathy** as they understand the perspectives of their teammates and appreciate their contributions to the project.

During construction, the child encounters unexpected problems, requiring self-control to manage frustration and stay focused. This **self-control** also allows them to regulate their impulses and avoid distractions, leading to a more efficient workflow.

Their **curiosity** propels them to explore different design possibilities and materials, leading to flexible thinking. They adapt to new information, experiment with alternative approaches, and embrace creative solutions to unforeseen challenges.

As the project nears completion, they encounter a setback—a crucial piece is missing. **Optimism** encourages them not to give up but to find alternative solutions. They brainstorm ideas with their peers, demonstrating **flexible thinking** in finding a workaround.

In the end, the model airplane stands as a testament to the interconnectedness of these attributes. *Persistence, precise communication, self-control, empathy, curiosity, flexible thinking, and optimism* have worked harmoniously to guide the child through the journey of creation, fostering growth and development at every step.

Chapter Structure

As we move forward into Chapters 2 through 8, we'll delve deeper into the 7 *Essential Attributes* that nurture confidence in our children. Each chapter will follow a consistent format: beginning with a thought-provoking quote, I'll define the attribute and then share stories or anecdotes highlighting its significance. We'll explore various ways parents can introduce or provide opportunities for their children to engage with each attribute, followed by reflection questions designed for parents. Finally, each chapter will offer practical steps parents can take immediately to teach and model the attribute in their everyday lives.

Chapter 9, Hopes and Dreams, will conclude the book by bringing to light the stories of parents and their children. This chapter encapsulates the essence of parental aspirations and integrates the collective wisdom of those who have shared their experiences. It celebrates the shared parenting journey and underscores the belief that every child can have a limitless and fulfilled future through love, support, and access to numerous opportunities.

CHAPTER 2

Fostering Persistence

"Nothing in this world can take the place of persistence. Talent will not; nothing is more common than unsuccessful people with talent. Genius will not; unrewarded genius is almost a proverb. Education will not; the world is full of educated derelicts. Persistence and determination alone are omnipotent. The slogan 'Press On!' has solved and always will solve the problems of the human race."

—Calvin Coolidge[38]

Persistence means not giving up when faced with a challenge. It is the ability to stick with a difficult task and cope with frustration.

In *Every Student Deserves a Gifted Education,* I wrote a story about a girl I pseudonymously named Stella. It was based on a real girl and her family. The story revolves around Stella's development of the element of persisting within a growth mindset. It is essential to share Stella's story here because it is highly relevant and clearly illustrates what teaching and modeling persistence looks like in real-life situations.

---

38 Calvin Coolidge, "Nothing in this world can take the place of persistence," Goodreads, https://www.goodreads.com/quotes/2749-nothing-in-this-world-can-take-the-place-of-persistence, accessed May 25, 2024.

REVISITING STELLA

"Stella, you are so talented. I know you will always do well!"
"So telling children they're smart, in the end, made them feel dumber, but claim they were smarter. I don't think this is what we're aiming for when we put positive labels—'gifted,' 'talented,' and 'brilliant'—on people. We don't mean to rob them of their zest for challenge and their recipes for Success.... This is the danger of positive labels."
—Carol Dweck

Stella's parents had a laid-back approach, aiming to give her every opportunity they could afford. At nine, Stella displayed exceptional golf skills, not because she was inherently more gifted than other children who had never played, but due to her opportunities and extensive practice with the feedback she had received. Stella's golf journey began when her father placed a putter in her hands at two years of age. Subsequently, she started accompanying her father and older brother to the golf range.

Stella found joy in hitting golf balls, and being around her family made it even more special. By the time she reached six or seven years old, it was estimated that Stella had hit over ten thousand golf balls on the range and practiced putting a golf ball thousands of times. Eventually, her parents arranged for Stella to have a coach. Stella, who had some perfectionistic tendencies and disliked making mistakes or losing, might have developed this mindset from wanting to match the skill level of her brother, who was four years older.

Around the same time, when Stella was six or seven, her parents enrolled her in mini-golf tournaments. Before her first tournament, Stella felt highly anxious, and, unfortunately, she finished in last place. This outcome devastated her as she believed she did not live up to the positive label of being "so talented" that everyone had given her since she started playing golf. Stella considered quitting the sport.

Put yourself in Stella's parents' shoes and reflect on the following questions.

What are some reasons (without placing blame) for Stella's meltdown?

What could have been done to support Stella's perfectionistic tendencies?

What can be done now to support Stella?

The Rest of the Story

Stella's parents recognized the need to act. They did not want her to quit golf, but they didn't want to force her to play either. They understood her love for the sport and wanted to equip her with the necessary tools to **persevere**. They introduced her to the concept of a growth mindset, aiming to help her embrace challenges and view them as opportunities for improvement. Stella's parents believed that **persisting** was a valuable life skill and a skill applicable to golf. They wanted her to understand that effort would lead to improvement. Learning from feedback provided by her coach, parents, peers, and herself would help her progress. Moreover, observing successful golfers, including her brother and father, would be positive models for her golfing journey. They shared videos with Stella, helping her comprehend the game of golf and learn from the perseverance and practice exhibited by other accomplished golfers in tournaments. Stella's parents clarified that their only desire was for her to find happiness and enjoyment in the game. They emphasized that focused and enjoyable practice would lead to more enjoyment as she improved.

As mentioned in the previous chapter, neurotransmitters in the brain affect our emotions. When Stella wanted to quit, cortisol, the stress hormone, was activated, likely putting her in flight mode. The objective was to activate her prefrontal cortex, the part of the brain responsible for critical thinking and decision-making, to trigger the release of "happy chemicals." By **persisting** and practicing, Stella would experience the positive feelings associated with dopamine and other "happy chemicals."

Stella's parents continued to guide her, assuring her that it was acceptable not to succeed every time. They taught her about the brain and introduced breathing exercises to help her calm her mind. Her coach taught her visualization techniques and mental rehearsal of golf shots, encouraging positive thinking about the outcomes. They helped her understand the challenges that amateur and professional golfers face. Stella's parents and coach showed her videos of professional golfers making mistakes and how they responded. They also took her to a professional women's golf tournament. They worked with her on a process of reflection, a quick analysis of mistakes, correcting them, and moving on to the next shot.

Due to the observation of Stella's perfectionistic tendencies in other areas, her parents sought assistance from the school. Fortunately, the school had recently adopted a growth mindset philosophy and had begun teaching it to all students. Stella's parents inquired if any techniques used in school could support Stella in golf and at home. The school provided them with talking points and sentence frames focused on persisting, assisting her when she felt anxious or believed she could not overcome challenges because they seemed too difficult.

Persistence Sentence Frames for Stella

I like that you took on that challenging golf hole, Stella.

I am excited to see you stretching yourself and working to improve your putting.

I admire the way you concentrated after that unfortunate shot.

You put so much thought into this.

The passion and effort you put into practicing and improving bring me joy. How do you feel about it?

Whoops, practicing putting from this short distance was too easy. I apologize for wasting your time. Let's increase the distance so you can truly master putts from four to six feet.

I can see how hard you are working. You must feel proud of yourself.

Your dedication to practicing with the 3-wood and driver is commendable.

I appreciate your effort, but let's continue working together to make your short irons more consistent.

It may take more time to become comfortable hitting a fairway wood, but you'll get there with persistence.

Every athlete has a unique approach to the game of golf. Let's keep trying to find the strategy that works best for you.

I'm proud of your commitment to improvement.

It upsets me when you don't finish what you started. Nobody hits a great shot every time or wins all matches, but finishing is important.

We can tackle challenging tasks.

This dedicated effort in teaching Stella about her brain and the growth mindset, particularly the idea of embracing persistence in the face of challenge, began to yield positive results. Stella developed a much more positive outlook on golf and started enjoying the hard work that came with it. She embraced playing and improving in tournaments, focusing less on her score and less on winning. Something unique started to happen: Stella became a role model for her peers on the course, gently helping them with their mindsets using the Growth Mindset Sentence Statements the adults had used with her. As a result, Stella began winning a few tournaments and even received an invitation to a major junior tournament because of her positive attitude and solid play.

To conclude Stella's story, let us reference another quote from Carol Dweck: *"I think educators commonly hold two beliefs that do just that. Many believe that (1) praising students' intelligence builds their confidence and motivation to learn, and (2) students' inherent intelligence is the major cause of their achievement in school. Our research has shown that the first belief is false and that the second can be harmful—even for the most competent students."*[39]

LANGUAGE OF PERSISTENCE: A JOURNEY TO FLUENCY

At my previous school, Mason Crest, we welcomed students from thirty-five different birth countries, each bringing a rich tapestry of cultural and linguistic diversity. Among them, we heard forty-two different languages, including English. The experience of being surrounded by such linguistic variety underscored the value of learning a second language. But how does this endeavor connect to the essential attribute of persistence?

Consider the story of Maria, a student at Mason Crest. Maria arrived at the school with little knowledge of English, having grown up speaking Spanish at home. Initially, she struggled to communicate effectively with some classmates and teachers. However, Maria possessed a deep-seated optimism and unwavering commitment to mastering English. If you knew Maria's parents, you would immediately

---

39 Carol Dweck, "The Perils and Promise of Praise," ASCD, October 1, 2007, https://www.ascd.org/el/articles/the-perils-and-promises-of-praise.

understand why. They modeled these behaviors in their lives at home, and Maria came to school understanding the value of persistence.

Despite the challenges she faced, Maria was not alone. She received dedicated support from various quarters at Mason Crest. Our English Language teacher team, classroom teachers, and other staff members rallied around Maria, providing extra practice sessions and scaffolded support tailored to her needs. Together, they ensured she had the resources and encouragement necessary to navigate the complexities of learning a new language.

Maria persisted, attending extra practice sessions, seeking out conversation partners, and diligently practicing her English skills every day. Slowly but surely, her efforts began to bear fruit. Slowly, Maria gained confidence in her ability to express herself in English.

However, Maria's journey was not without setbacks. There were moments of frustration and doubt when she felt like giving up. Yet, fueled by her unwavering optimism and determination, Maria pressed on. She viewed every obstacle as an opportunity to learn and grow, refusing to let setbacks deter her from her goal.

Over time, Maria's hard work paid off. She became fluent in English, could converse fluently with her peers, and participated actively in class discussions. More than just acquiring a new language, Maria had embraced a valuable skill set that would serve her well. Her success was a testament to the power of persistence and the joy of overcoming language barriers.

Maria's story is not unique at Mason Crest but exemplifies the school's ethos. Mason Crest instills in all students the growth mindset philosophy, emphasizing the value of embracing challenges and viewing effort as the pathway to mastery. This approach fosters a culture where persistence is celebrated, and every student is empowered to unleash their unlimited potential, regardless of obstacles.

THE POWER OF PERSISTENCE:
ALTHEA GIBSON'S LEGACY

As I was growing up in the late '60s and early '70s, my parents often shared stories about Black Americans who, in the face of injustice and racial prejudice, demonstrated remarkable persistence, including themselves. They emphasized that bitterness and victimhood were not the answer despite these challenges. Instead, they taught me that hard work and unwavering focus on one's goals could lead to success. One such figure who embodied this spirit was Althea Gibson, who was frequently mentioned in our household. Her story resonated with me deeply, especially since tennis, my favorite sport, was central to her achievements. Alongside her, Arthur Ashe stood out as a beacon of perseverance, reinforcing that persistence is a crucial quality for everyone to embrace.

Althea Gibson's journey was not just about breaking racial barriers in tennis but also about challenging societal norms. In an era marred by racial segregation and prejudice, she stepped onto the tennis court and changed the game. As a pioneering Black tennis player, Gibson shattered the color barrier in professional tennis and challenged prevailing gender roles. Her remarkable journey, filled with unique challenges and triumphs, is a testament to her strength and determination, making her story an apt illustration of persistence for this section.

Born on August 25, 1927, in Silver, South Carolina, Gibson grew up in a time with limited opportunities. Seeking a better life, her family moved to Harlem, where her love for sports, particularly tennis, would eventually lead to unprecedented success and historical significance. At thirteen, Althea started playing paddle tennis on the streets of Harlem. Her talent was noticed by Buddy Walker, a director of the Police Athletic League, who encouraged her to play on public courts. There, she drew the attention of Fred Johnson, a renowned one-armed tennis coach, who taught her the game and set her on a path to professional competition.

Gibson's hunger for competing at the highest levels grew as her skills developed. In 1950, she made history as the first African American to compete in the United States National Championships (now the US Open), directly challenging the segregation in American sports. This groundbreaking debut was just the beginning. In 1956, she became the first African American to win a Grand Slam title at the French Championships (now the French Open).

Althea Gibson's career reached its pinnacle in 1957 when she won both Wimbledon and the US National Championships, becoming the first Black person to achieve this feat. Her success was not just personal; it also marked a significant shift in the sport. She continued her dominance in 1958 by defending both titles, cementing her status as a tennis legend. Throughout her illustrious career, Gibson captured eleven Grand Slam titles in singles, doubles, and mixed doubles competitions. She later transitioned to professional golf, becoming the first Black woman to join the Ladies Professional Golf Association (LPGA).

Althea Gibson's impact extended far beyond her athletic achievements. She played a significant role in the fight for racial equality, paving the way for future generations of African American athletes. Her influence can be seen in the careers of icons like the late Arthur Ashe, Venus Williams, and Serena Williams, all of whom have acknowledged her profound impact on their lives and careers.

Althea Gibson's legacy continues to resonate today, reminding us of the power of perseverance. Her story is a powerful example of how persistence can lead to extraordinary achievements, inspiring our children to pursue their dreams with determination and resilience.[40]

---

40 Adapted from Otherwise Inc., "Figures of Speech: The Althea Gibson Story," https://www.otherwiseinc.com/blog/figures-of-speech-the-althea-gibson-story/, accessed June 10, 2024.

In the article "The Psychology Behind Persistence: Understanding Traits and Motivations" published on Medium.com by MS-HuecoDev on December 7, 2023, the author explores the intricate psychology of persistence. They highlight motivation as the driving force, emphasizing intrinsic and extrinsic factors. Resilience, grit, and a growth mindset are crucial for sustaining persistence, delaying gratification, and effectively managing emotions. Additionally, a supportive social environment significantly influences one's ability to persist through challenges. Ultimately, individuals can develop the determination to overcome obstacles and achieve their goals by cultivating these traits and motivations.[41]

Providing Other Opportunities/Experiences for Parents to Teach Persistence

Martial Arts Classes: Many martial arts traditions incorporate elements of discipline and perseverance that are culturally diverse and can resonate with children from various backgrounds.

Musical Instrument Lessons: Music is a universal language, and children from diverse cultural backgrounds can find instruments and musical styles that resonate with their heritage, encouraging persistence in learning.

Reflection Questions for Parents

How can you encourage persistence in your child's endeavors without adding undue pressure?

Reflect on a time when your child faced a setback. How did you support them in persisting through the challenge?

---

41 MS-HuecoDev, "The Psychology Behind Persistence: Understanding Traits and Motivations," Medium, December 7, 2023, https://medium.com/p/the-psychology-behind-persistence-understanding-traits-and-motivations-7b8f3a42a791.

What strategies can you employ to model persistence and serve as a positive example for your child?

Consider your child's strengths and areas for growth. How can you help them develop persistence in areas where they may struggle?

Are there people your child looks up to whose story of persistence would resonate?

What Parents Can Do Today

In her article *6 Evidence-Based Ways to Encourage Persistence in Children*, published in *Psychology Today* on August 30, 2021, Cara Goodwin, PhD, offers practical strategies for parents to instill persistence in their children.

1. Avoid Taking Over: Resist the temptation to step in and complete tasks for your child when they become difficult. Instead, offer verbal assistance only when requested, allowing them space to problem-solve independently.

2. Model Persistence: Share personal stories of overcoming challenges, highlighting the role of effort in achieving success. By modeling persistence, parents demonstrate its importance in tackling difficult tasks.

3. Break Tasks Down: Help children break complex tasks into smaller, manageable steps or set incremental goals to facilitate progress. This approach reduces the feeling of being overwhelmed and empowers children to tackle challenges one step at a time.

4. Utilize Process Praise: Focus on praising the effort rather than just the outcomes. Acknowledge and celebrate the hard work and determination children put into their tasks, reinforcing the value of persistence.

5. Acknowledge Persistence: Recognize and praise children when they persist in difficult tasks, even if it involves questioning authority. By validating their efforts, parents encourage continued perseverance.

6. Encourage Exploration: Encourage children to explore new and challenging activities that align with their interests. Children develop resilience and perseverance by stepping outside their comfort zones and embracing challenges.

By incorporating these evidence-based strategies into parenting practices, caregivers can effectively nurture persistence and resilience in children, equipping them with valuable skills to overcome obstacles and achieve success.[42]

42 Cara Goodwin, PhD, "6 Evidence-Based Ways to Encourage Persistence in Children," *Psychology Today*, August 30, 2021, https://shorturl.at/bfhGN.

CHAPTER 3

Nurturing Precise Communication

"If people had the right skills and intention to communicate well, there would be no conflict. The better we are at communicating, the better our lives will be."

—Yama Mubtaker[43]

Precise communication (oral and written) enables children to express themselves clearly and effectively in all aspects of life.

Our children must be clear in written, verbal, and listening skills in a world of texting, sound bites, clickbait, and a lack of seemingly sustained focus on precise communication. As renowned educator Mike Schmoker (2004) asserted, "Clarity Precedes Competence."[44]

FROM CONFUSION TO CLARITY: THE IMPORTANCE OF PRECISE COMMUNICATION

Anybody who knows me knows I detest acronyms when people use them without checking to see if others understand what they're talking about. I remember when I first became a teacher. In my first year, during

---

43 Daniel Ndukwu, "50 Quotes About Communication to Deliver Better Messages," Chanty, October 17, 2023, https://www.chanty.com/blog/communication-quotes/, accessed May 26, 2024.
44 Mike Schmoker, "Learning Communities at a Crossroads: A Response to Joyce and Cook. *Phi Delta Kappan*, 2004, 86(1), 84-89.

a staff meeting, numerous acronyms were used. Being a new teacher and not wanting to call attention to myself, I was completely lost. I had no idea what my colleagues were discussing.

Communication should be all about clarity and the effective exchange of information and ideas. The sender must simplify their message to ensure it is received. Whether in verbal or written form, clarity precedes competence. You cannot move forward as an individual, a team, or an organization if everyone is not on the same page regarding their understanding of what has been communicated.

Throughout my career, I constantly asked for clarification whenever I encountered acronyms or jargon I didn't understand. Once I gathered the courage, I would say, "What does that mean? I'm not clear." A lack of clarity stops learning and creates confusion. That's why I'm so passionate about precise communication. Our children can gain credibility and avoid frustration and conflict if they share and receive information accurately.

Precise communication also involves listening and clarifying when you don't understand something. It's about seeking understanding if you're unclear on what's being communicated. But it's also the communicator's responsibility to be self-aware and socially aware. They need to consider who is in the room and the audience's varying levels of understanding. A good communicator asks, "Who may not understand what I'm saying? How can I communicate this message as simply as possible?"

As an administrator, my mantra was that common language, common knowledge, and common expectations create common understanding. Using big words or jargon may make the communicator feel important, but it doesn't help with clarity and understanding. When working with our children, we must be aware of their developmental levels and help them develop precise communication skills—both written and verbal.

We need to teach, model, and reinforce the idea that they must communicate clearly if they want to be understood and avoid frustration.

I sometimes speak faster than I should and must remind myself that people might not understand me the first time. It's not their fault; I might not be articulating clearly, speaking too quickly, or slurring my words, which frustrates the listener.

In today's world, filled with sound bites, short clips, texts, memes, and symbols, we must help our children understand that to be understood, they must be self-aware about how they communicate and socially aware of their audience. They need to ensure their message is received and understood clearly.

WHO'S ON FIRST?

Any productive learning, as well as positive relationships, is built on clear and precise communication. When I was a young boy, I can remember watching my black-and-white television in the early 1970s (yes, I am old), watching a comedy routine by the famous comedy duo Abbott and Costello.

In their famous sketch "Who's on First?" Abbott and Costello create a humorous scenario where the confusion of words highlights the importance of precise communication. The routine plays on the ambiguity of the words "Who," "What," and "I Don't Know," which are used as player names. Here's a simplified breakdown of the skit to illustrate the point:

Abbott: Well, Costello, I'm going to New York with you. Bucky Harris, the Yankees manager, gave me a job as a coach for as long as you're on the team.

Costello: Look, Abbott, if you're the coach, you must know all the players.

Abbott: I certainly do.

Costello: Well, you know I've never met the guys. So you'll have to tell me their names, and then I'll know who's playing on the team.

Abbott: Oh, I'll tell you their names, but you know it seems to me they give these ballplayers nowadays very peculiar names.

Costello: You mean funny names?

Abbott: Strange names, pet names...like Dizzy Dean...

Costello: His brother Daffy...

Abbott: Daffy Dean...

Costello: And their French cousin...

Abbott: French?

Costello: Goofe' Dean.

Abbott: Well, let's see, we have on the bags, Who's on first, What's on second, I Don't Know is on third...

Costello: That's what I want to find out.

Abbott: I say Who's on first, What's on second, I Don't Know's on third.

Costello: Are you the manager?

Abbott: Yes.

Costello: You gonna be the coach too?

Abbott: Yes.

Costello: And you don't know the fellows' names?

Abbott: Well, I should.

Costello: Well, then, who's on first?

Abbott: Yes.

Costello: I mean the fellow's name.

Abbott: Who!

Costello: The guy on first.

Abbott: Who!

Costello: The first baseman.

Abbott: Who!

Costello: The guy playing...

Abbott: Who is on first!

Costello: I'm asking you who's on first?

Abbott: That's the man's name.

Costello: That's whose name?

Abbott: Yes.

Costello: Well, go ahead and tell me.

Abbott: That's it.

Costello: That's who?

Abbott: Yes.

This back-and-forth exchange continues, emphasizing how miscommunication and the lack of precise clarity can lead to confusion. Abbott and Costello's routine humorously demonstrates that conversations can go in circles without clear and precise communication, leading to misunderstandings. This skit remains a classic example of why clarity is essential in all forms of communication, especially in a rapidly evolving digital world where precision can prevent miscommunication and foster better understanding.

The humor of Abbott and Costello's "Who's on First?" routine not only entertains but also serves as a valuable lesson in the importance of clarity in communication.[45]

THE TELEPHONE GAME

A simple yet powerful demonstration of the importance of clear communication is the "telephone game." In this game, participants sit in a circle, and one person whispers a message to the next person. This continues around the circle until the last person shares the message. The final message is often hilariously different from the original, illustrating how easily information can become distorted through unclear communication.

By nurturing precise communication skills in children, we are equipping them with essential tools for their future academic, social, and professional lives.

Why Are Precise Communication Skills So Critical in All Aspects of Life?

Precise communication skills are vital for success in education, career development, job interviews, and personal interactions. Shakuntala Vidyalaya's article highlights the significant impact of conversational

---

45 "Original Who's on First," Parkway Schools, https://www.parkwayschools.net/cms/lib/MO01931486/Centricity/Domain/1578/Original-whos_on_first.pdf, accessed July 8, 2024.

skills on various aspects of life and why students need to develop these abilities. Here are the main reasons why communication skills are crucial for students, as outlined in the article:

1. **Enhancing Learning:** Many students hesitate to ask questions due to fear, hesitation, and low confidence. Strong communication skills help students to listen and understand their teachers' points of view. This understanding enables students to ask better questions confidently, thereby gaining more knowledge.

2. **Improving Job Prospects:** Clear communication skills, confident physical expressions, and the ability to use objective vocabulary during interviews significantly improve students' chances of securing jobs after graduation. Effective communication enhances students' personalities, making them more attractive to potential employers.

3. **Fostering Teamwork and Collaboration:** Effective communication is critical to business productivity. It improves one's chances of promotion and earning colleague respect, enhances teamwork, and fosters a collaborative attitude. These skills are invaluable for long-term professional success.

4. **Engaging Socially:** Respectful and effective communication is essential in social interactions. Students must learn to communicate without distressing others, which helps build trust and self-esteem. Healthy communication with parents, teachers, classmates, and others positively impacts students' education and personal growth.

5. **Enhancing Cognitive Skills:** Good communication skills sharpen students' minds and memory. Effective communication

practices increase focus and readiness, improving vocabulary, communication skills, and memory retention. These cognitive benefits contribute to academic and personal success.

Developing these skills helps students succeed in their studies and careers and fosters better relationships and social interactions.[46] [47]

Providing other Opportunities/Experiences for Parents to Teach Precise Communication

Debate Team: Structured debates can include topics relevant to various cultural perspectives, allowing children to express themselves precisely and their viewpoints effectively.

Writing Workshops: Writing workshops can explore storytelling traditions from different cultures, encouraging children to communicate precisely while honoring diverse narrative styles and voices.

Cooking Classes: Offering cooking classes where parents and children learn recipes from different cultures can provide an opportunity for precise communication. Parents can teach their children about specific ingredients, techniques, and cultural significance, fostering clear communication while bonding over shared culinary experiences.

Language Exchange Groups: Creating language exchange groups where parents and children can interact with speakers of different languages can enhance precise communication skills. Through conversation and cultural exchange, participants can learn to express themselves

46 Shakuntala Vidyalaya, "Why Students Lack Communication Skills?" Medium, May 7, 2019, https://medium.com/@shakuntalavidyalaya/why-students-lack-communication-skills, accessed May 26, 2024.
47 SV School Group. "How to Improve Communication Skills of Students," Medium, https://medium.com/@svschoolgroup/how-to-improve-communication-skills-of-students-d6ae2b9e209f, accessed May 26, 2024.

accurately in various languages while gaining insights into different communication styles and cultural nuances.

Community Library Events: Many local libraries offer free or low-cost events and programs for families, such as storytelling sessions, language clubs, or cultural workshops. Parents and children can attend these events together, engaging in activities that promote precise communication and cultural understanding without financial burden.

Nature Walks and Exploration: Exploring nature together can be an enriching experience for parents and children, fostering communication and appreciation for the world around them. Nature walks, birdwatching, or simply spending time in local parks provide opportunities for parents to teach precise communication skills while connecting with their children and the environment, all at no cost.

Reflection Questions for Parents

1. Reflect on when you felt confused due to unclear communication. How did it affect your understanding and response in that situation?

2. How do you ensure clarity when communicating with your children? Are there specific strategies you use to make sure they understand you?

3. How can we create daily opportunities for our children to practice storytelling at home, encouraging them to use descriptive language and clearly express their ideas?

4. How do you model precise communication for your children? Can you identify any habits you have that might hinder clear communication (e.g., speaking too quickly or using jargon)?

5. Do your children feel comfortable asking for clarification when they

don't understand something? How do you create an environment where they feel safe to ask questions?

6. How do you demonstrate active listening when your children speak to you? What techniques do you use to show that you are engaged and understand their messages?

7. When explaining complex ideas or instructions to your children, how do you simplify the message to ensure they grasp it fully?

8. How do you encourage your children to give and receive feedback on their communication? What methods do you use to help them improve their skills?

9. How can we integrate specific vocabulary related to various topics into our daily interactions, encouraging our children to use precise language in speaking and writing?

10. How can we organize family debates or discussions on various topics that require our children to present their ideas clearly and support them with well-structured arguments?

What Parents Can Do Today

1. Storytelling Sessions: Engage your child in a daily storytelling activity. Encourage them to narrate a story or recount their day using descriptive language. Prompt them to include specific details about characters, settings, and events to help them practice clear and precise expression.

2. Family Discussions: Initiate small group discussions during meals or family gatherings. Model active listening by paraphrasing your child's words before responding and encouraging them to do the same. This practice will help them learn to respond with clarity and precision.

3. Vocabulary Building: Choose a "word of the day" related to different subjects and use it in sentences throughout the day. Encourage your child to use this new vocabulary in their conversations and writing. This will help them learn to incorporate precise language in their communication.

4. Structured Debates with Quality Talk:

- Organize a friendly family debate on a topic of interest. Help your child prepare by discussing the importance of presenting clear and well-structured arguments.

- Teach your children the concept of "quality talk" and how to debate respectfully using sentence starters such as:

Acknowledging Others' Ideas

"Thanks for explaining that, _____."

"That's a great idea, _____."

"_____, you did a nice job on _____."

Adding to Someone Else's Thinking

"I agree because _____."

"I think another reason is _____."

Explaining Disagreements

"I disagree because _____."

"That idea doesn't make sense because _____."

"Could you explain that again?"

"I don't understand the part about _____."

"How did you figure that out?"

Getting More Information and Asking for Proof

"Why do you think that?"

"Where is that in the text?"

"Can you give an example?"

Recapping Important Information

"So far, we decided _____."

"We already know that _____."

"So, what you're saying is _____."

Getting Everyone Involved

"Can anyone add to that idea?"

"What do you think, _____?"

"Who else noticed something about _____?"[48]

Using these strategies and sentence starters, you can help your child learn to debate respectfully and articulate their thoughts clearly, enhancing their precise communication skills. Of course, you should choose developmentally appropriate material for your child's age. Additionally, the questions can be adapted to accommodate family size and structure.

---

48 Beth Hillerns, Accountable Talk Posters, 2011, http://qualityeducator.net.

CHAPTER 4

Developing Self-Control

*"Research shows that willpower is more important than IQ.
That's why the point isn't to become smarter
but to become more self-disciplined."*
—Adam Kirk Smith[49]

Self-control involves managing emotions and impulses, making informed choices, and maintaining composure in challenging situations.

CLINT, YOU ARE NOT A PROBLEM; YOU ARE A DRUMMER: A GIFT HIDING IN PLAIN SIGHT

Clint Pulver tells his story of how his perceived lack of self-control got him in trouble when he was an elementary school student, but his teacher saw it as his gift:

> I have a lot of memories from when I was a child. One that's always stuck out to me, though, was when I was about ten years old. I was in school, and I struggled. I didn't struggle with English, math, or science. I struggled with holding still. I would try to listen and focus and process ideas, but I couldn't help myself. To be honest, I would sit there and then just start tapping. The students in the class would look at me and say, "Hey, stop tapping." A lot of

49 "Adam Kirk Smith," Goodreads, https://www.goodreads.com/author/quotes/15976168.Adam_Kirk_Smith, accessed June 1, 2024.

the time, I didn't even realize I was doing it. Eventually, even the teachers got after me. They would yell at me and say, "Clint, you have to stop tapping." It got so bad that I got sent to the principal's office for tapping. He said to me, "Clint, when you go back to class, just try sitting on your hands." So I did. I went back to class, and when I felt myself starting to tap, I sat on my hands. That worked for about five seconds.

One time, I was tapping in class, and my teacher, Mr. Jensen, looked at me and yelled, "Clint, stay after class." I thought to myself, "This is it. I am done." I've always been the type of person that believes a single moment in time can change a person's life, and this was one of those moments for me. I will never forget it. I was sitting there with Mr. Jensen in an empty classroom. He walked past me and sat next to his desk. He said, "Clint, come here. I need to talk to you." As he looked me right in the eye, he said, "You're not in trouble, but I do have just one question that I have to ask you." He asked, "Have you ever thought about playing the drums?"

In that moment, Mr. Jensen leaned back, opened the top drawer of his desk, and pulled out my very first pair of drumsticks. He held them in his hands and looked at me. He said, "Clint, you're not a problem. I think you're a drummer." From that moment on, I've never put those sticks down. I've toured, recorded, and played drums all over the world. My whole college education was paid for with drumsticks in my hand, all because of a single moment in time when somebody believed in me. He saw something in me that I didn't even see within myself. From that moment, I learned that there's a difference between being the best in the world and being the best for the world.[50]

---

50 ClintPulver.com, http://www.ClintPulver.com, accessed June 1, 2024.

REGINA'S DISCIPLINE AND SELF-CONTROL

From the beginning, Regina's parents were determined to give her every opportunity to explore and grow. As Regina grew, her parents ensured she was exposed to diverse experiences. They took her to museums, parks, and cultural events, opening her eyes to the world's richness. They also enrolled her in various extracurricular activities, from sports to music lessons, allowing her to discover her interests.

Regina's days were filled with new adventures and challenges throughout her childhood. She threw herself into each activity with gusto, eager to learn and grow. Whether painting in art class, kicking a soccer ball on the field, or playing a musical instrument, Regina approached each opportunity with an open mind and a willingness to try her best.

As Regina entered her teenage years, her interests began to crystallize. She found herself drawn to the performing arts, spending hours rehearsing for school plays and musical performances. She also developed a passion for technology, spending countless hours tinkering with computers and learning to code.

With the support of her family and the opportunities available, Regina's passion continued to flourish. She worked hard in school, excelling in her chosen subjects and participating in extracurricular activities that fueled her interests. As she reached adulthood, Regina was well on her way to pursuing her dreams, armed with a wealth of experiences and a burning passion to make her mark on the world.

While growing up, Regina's parents instilled in her a love for exploration and the importance of self-discipline and self-control. They also emphasized the value of patience, perseverance, and restraint from a young age.

In her early years, Regina learned the art of delayed gratification through simple yet effective practices. Whether waiting her turn during a game with friends or saving her allowance to buy a coveted toy, she discovered the power of restraint in pursuing long-term goals.

Her parents led by example, modeling patience and self-control in their own lives. They taught Regina to take a step back and consider the consequences of her actions, encouraging her to think before acting and to make thoughtful decisions.

As Regina grew older, her parents continued reinforcing these lessons, providing opportunities for her to practice self-discipline in various aspects of her life. Whether sticking to a practice schedule for her piano lessons or maintaining a regular study routine for school, Regina learned that success often required sacrifice and dedication.

Through it all, Regina's parents offered guidance and support, praising her efforts and offering supportive correction when needed. They celebrated her successes but also helped her navigate setbacks, teaching her resilience in the face of adversity.

By the time Regina reached adulthood, she had internalized these lessons of self-control and discipline, carrying them with her as she pursued her passions and faced life's challenges. Armed with a strong sense of self-regulation, Regina approached each new opportunity with confidence and composure, knowing she had the skills and determination to succeed.

IMPOSSIBLE IS ONLY SOMEONE ELSE'S PERCEPTION

Serena Williams is considered by most to be the best women's tennis player in history. Her will, determination, and persistence are well-documented. Here is her one-time coach, Patrick Mouratoglou, sharing a story of her displaying these attributes:

> There are so many examples of incredible things Serena's achieved, but one always stands out for me. It was during Roland Garros.

She was very sick; she had a fever. She couldn't even get out of bed. She didn't practice at all; she didn't leave the bed at all. She could not. She was just going from the bed to the tennis court to play her match at Roland Garros and then come back home. She won the tournament without being able to practice, warm up for the matches, or even walk. A few times I came to her apartment, I said, "Come with me, let's walk a little bit, take some fresh air." She couldn't stand up; she was too weak, so she had to go back to bed. But she was able to win matches.

Impossible, impossible. Her will to win was so strong, and her refusal to lose was also so strong that she was finding resources that probably nobody else on this planet would have found. What Serena taught me is that what people perceive as reality is just what they see; it's not the reality. The reality is what you're able to achieve. So a lot of times, people would say, "This is impossible." This thing being impossible is their perception of what is the reality. But when Serena did it, the reality became that it was possible.[51]

Delayed Gratification Self-Control

People who can delay gratification resist the temptation of immediate rewards to achieve long-term goals. This requires much self-control and discipline, but it is a key trait of successful and persistent individuals.[52]

---

51 "Impossible is Only Someone Else's Perception," Instagram post, https://www.instagram.com/reel/C78-KOEN3eS/?igsh=djYobTZuc2gyd2dm, accessed July 10, 2024.
52 "The Psychology Behind Persistence: Understanding the Determination to Overcome Challenges," MS-HuecoDev, December 7, 2023, https://medium.com/@mshuecodev/the-psychology-behind-persistence-understanding-the-determination-to-overcome-challenges-e085c5b9cfd0.

Other Opportunities/Experiences
for Parents to Teach Self-Control

Martial Arts Classes: Many martial arts disciplines emphasize self-control and discipline, drawing on cultural traditions worldwide, such as karate from Japan, taekwondo from Korea, or capoeira from Brazil.

Yoga Classes: Yoga originated in ancient India and promoted self-awareness, deep breathing, stretching, and self-control, making it culturally relevant to children from diverse backgrounds.

Reflection Questions for Parents

1. How do you model self-control in your behavior, and how might your actions influence your child's understanding and practice of self-control?

2. In what ways do you currently support your child in managing their emotions and impulses, and are there areas where you could enhance this support?

3. How do you handle situations where your child displays impulsivity or struggles with self-regulation, and how might you adjust your approach to nurture their self-control skills better?

4. Reflecting on your upbringing, what lessons about self-control do you recall learning from your parents or caregivers, and how do those lessons shape your parenting practices today?

What Parents Can Do Today

1. Establish Consistent Routines and Boundaries: Children thrive on predictability, which can help them develop self-control by helping them understand expectations and consequences.

2. Teach Emotional Awareness and Regulation Techniques: Help your child identify and express their emotions in healthy ways, such as through breathing exercises, journaling, or discussing feelings openly.

3. Encourage Delayed Gratification: Foster patience and self-discipline by providing opportunities for your child to wait for rewards or privileges, whether it's delaying dessert until after dinner or saving allowance money for a desired toy.

4. Model Self-Control Behaviors: Your actions should demonstrate patience, impulse control, and emotional regulation. Children often learn best by observing and imitating the behavior of adults around them.

5. Offer Praise and Positive Reinforcement: Acknowledge and celebrate instances when your child demonstrates self-control, reinforcing the value of their efforts and encouraging continued growth in this area.

CHAPTER 5

Building Empathy

"What people of all ages can use in a moment of distress is not agreement or disagreement; they need someone to recognize what it is they're experiencing."
—Adele Faber[53]

Empathy allows children to understand and share the feelings of others, fostering meaningful relationships and a sense of social responsibility.

MY EMPATHY LESSON: A PARENT'S REFLECTION

"To know the road ahead, ask those coming back."
—Chinese Proverb[54]

I've always considered myself empathetic, stemming from my struggles as a learner in my youth. However, there was one instance in my early twenties when I failed to show empathy at all.

Our lack of empathy can eventually come back to haunt us, reflecting the same lack of compassion we once exhibited. I use myself as an example because we're all susceptible to such lapses in understanding. Before Kathleen and I had children, we traveled extensively. During

---

53 Karen Gerten, "16 Quotes on Parenting With Empathy," June 25, 2022, https://www.youthdynamics.org/16-quotes-on-parenting-with-empathy/, accessed June 8, 2024.
54 Comunity of Minds. https://thecomonline.net/to-know-the-road-ahead-ask-those-coming-back-chinese-proverb/, accessed June 8, 2024.

that time, I must confess, I didn't give much thought to parents with young children.

On a flight to Europe, several kids were onboard, spanning various ages, from babies to teens. While most of the journey was uneventful, there were moments of crying and screaming, leaving their parents struggling to calm them down. I found it chaotic at the time and thought, "Why can't they just keep their kids quiet? This is so annoying!" It was a lack of empathy on my part—I failed to imagine the challenges of being a young parent.

Fast forward a few years, and we welcomed our first child, Alison. During a trip to Arizona and Nevada, Alison developed an ear infection, making the flight back excruciating. She cried almost the entire time, and we felt terrible for inconveniencing other passengers. We experienced firsthand the judgmental stares and wished we could disappear. My previous lack of empathy came back to haunt me.

A couple of years later, during a trip to Florida with Alison and our youngest daughter, Emily, Emily fell ill and vomited just before landing. Unfortunately, our gate was occupied, so we had to endure the wait with the smell of vomit lingering. However, a kind woman behind us reassured us, offering her support and understanding. Her empathy helped us relax despite the discomfort.

Now, as empty nesters, whenever I encounter parents struggling with young children on flights, I feel an overwhelming urge to comfort them. Having been through similar experiences, I want to reassure them that everything will be alright. Empathy is a powerful tool that we can all cultivate and share.

The idea that empathy cannot be taught is simply untrue. Nurturing empathy in children from an early age equips them to build stronger relationships and navigate the complexities of life with compassion and understanding. It's a gift that benefits them and those around them, fostering a sense of unity and belonging in our communities.

THE KINDEST PERSON IN THE ROOM
IS OFTEN THE SMARTEST

In a keynote address at Benedictine College (2023), Governor J. B. Pritzker of Illinois delivered a powerful message on the importance of kindness and empathy. His speech emphasizes that empathy is a form of intelligence and provides valuable insights that parents can use to instill empathy in their children.

> When we see someone who doesn't look like us, sound like us, act like us, love like us, or live like us, the first thought that crosses almost everyone's brain is rooted in either fear or judgment or both. That's evolution. We survived as a species by being suspicious of things that we aren't familiar with. In order to be kind, we have to shut down that animal instinct and force our brain to travel a different pathway. Empathy and compassion are evolved states of being. They require the mental capacity to step past our most primal urges.

> This may be a surprising assessment because somewhere along the way in the last few years, our society has come to believe that weaponized cruelty is part of some well-thought-out master plan. They never forced their animal brain to evolve past its first instinct. They never forged new mental pathways to overcome their own instinctual fears. And so, their thinking and problem-solving will lack the imagination and creativity that the kindest people have in spades.

> Over my many years in politics and business, I have found one thing to be universally true: the kindest person in the room is also the smartest.

Governor Pritzker's words emphasize the importance of teaching children to overcome their initial instincts of fear or judgment toward others who are different. By encouraging children to practice empathy and compassion, parents can help them develop the mental pathways necessary for kindness, fostering creativity and problem-solving skills. This example shows that empathy is not just a nice-to-have attribute but an essential component of intelligence and effective leadership.[55]

NURTURING COMPASSION FROM BIRTH TO GRADUATION—AMIR

Amir was born into a world of rich culture and heritage. From the moment he was born, his parents, Nadia and Kareem, made it their mission to instill in him the profound value of empathy.

As a baby, Amir was cradled in his parents' arms, surrounded by warmth and love. Nadia and Kareem spoke to him in soothing tones, teaching him to recognize emotions in their voices, expressions, and actions. They believed that empathy was not just a skill to be learned but a way of being—a fundamental aspect of humanity.

As Amir grew, so did his understanding of empathy. His parents didn't just tell him to be kind—they showed him. They volunteered together at soup kitchens and shelters for the unhoused, demonstrating the importance of lending a helping hand to those in need. They read books together about people from different backgrounds and cultures, fostering Amir's ability to see the world through others' eyes.

Amir's upbringing was filled with diverse experiences that broadened his perspective and deepened his empathy. His family traveled to different countries, immersing themselves in unfamiliar cultures and traditions. They attended community events and celebrations, where Amir learned to appreciate the beauty of diversity and the richness of human connection.

---

55 J. B. Pritzker, "Commencement Address: Kindness/Empathy is Intelligence," Benedictine College, June 28, 2023, https://www.youtube.com/watch?v=5uFwyPP5GOQ, accessed July 8, 2024.

Amir's parents encouraged him to befriend classmates from all walks of life in school. They taught him to listen actively and without judgment and to offer support and understanding to those who needed it most. As he grew older, they had conversations with him about social issues, helping him develop a sense of empathy not just for individuals but for entire communities and society.

By the time Amir graduated high school, empathy had become second nature. He was known among his peers as someone who could be counted on for a compassionate ear or a shoulder to lean on. As he looked toward the future, he knew that whatever path he chose, empathy would guide him, enriching his relationships and empowering him to make a positive difference in the world.

DOLLY PARTON: "IF YOU SEE SOMEONE WITHOUT A SMILE, GIVE THEM YOURS."

I've watched countless Dolly Parton movies and shows and listened to her songs since I was young. Although I'm not what you would call a fanatic, I have always admired her kind and empathetic spirit. It's clear that even though we only see celebrities from afar, there's something universally acknowledged about Dolly's kindness and empathy.

Dolly Parton is a singer, songwriter, actress, and the mastermind behind Dollywood. Her career has spanned over fifty years and is marked by talent, unique style, and countless hits. However, there is another superpower behind her success: empathy.

Parton's Secret? Empathy.

"I can relate to everybody about anything," Parton said in an interview. This ability to relate is crucial for her as a songwriter because she needs to keep her emotions visible and accessible. She said in a 2019 article, "Some people harden their hearts just to get through life, and I think if I do that, I won't be able to write. I try to keep my heart open, even to the point of having to suffer more because I take everything so personal. But that's why I can write for other people: I try to keep myself where they are."[56]

Dolly's empathy transcends the typical "know your audience" advice. True empathy involves loving others unconditionally. It's about engaging with them genuinely, understanding their struggles, and appreciating their humanity.

Dolly Parton's approach teaches us that genuine empathy combines understanding and unconditional love. By teaching your children to connect deeply with others, you help them navigate challenges for themselves in a way that resonates deeply with those around them. This empathetic approach is a powerful foundation for building positive relationships and their success and happiness in any field.

Providing Other Opportunities/Experiences for Parents to Teach Empathy

Community Service Projects: Community service projects can be tailored to address issues relevant to different cultural communities, fostering empathy and understanding among children from diverse backgrounds.

Theater Classes: Theater classes can explore plays and stories from various cultures, allowing children to empathize with characters and themes that reflect different lived experiences.

---

56 Alison Davis, "Dolly Parton Shares the Secret to Her Success (And It's Not What You Think)." Inc.com, January 15, 2019, https://www.inc.com/alison-davis/dolly-parton-shares-secret-to-her-success-and-its-not-what-you-think.html, accessed June 6, 2024.

Reflection Questions for Parents

1. How do you currently model empathy in your interactions with your children and others?

2. In what ways can you help your child recognize and understand emotions beyond just words, like how Nadia and Kareem did with Amir?

3. What opportunities are you providing for your child to engage with diverse cultures and perspectives within your family and the community?

4. How can you encourage your child to empathize with individuals and larger societal issues, as Amir's parents did through conversations about social issues; for example, homelessness?

5. Consider when you may have lacked empathy toward another parent or caregiver in a challenging situation. How did that experience influence your perspective on empathy, and how do you strive to cultivate empathy in yourself and your children now?

What Parents Can Do Today

1. **Model Empathy:** Show empathy in your interactions with your child, other family members, and community members. Acknowledge and validate their feelings.

2. **Engage in Volunteer Activities:** Find opportunities for your family to volunteer together, whether it's at a soup kitchen, a homeless shelter, or other community service projects. This hands-on experience can help children understand the importance of empathy in action.

3. **Explore Diverse Cultures:** Read books, watch movies, or attend cultural events together that expose your child to different cultures

and perspectives. Discuss what you learn and encourage your child to ask questions. Just like Dolly Parton learns something from every interaction, encourage your children to see every relationship as an opportunity for growth and learning. This continuous learning fuels genuine connection and personal development.

4. Foster Active Listening: Teach your child the importance of listening actively and without judgment. Encourage them to listen to others' perspectives and experiences openly.

5. Discuss Social Issues: Have age-appropriate conversations with your child about social issues and current events. Help them understand the impact of these issues on individuals and communities and encourage them to think about how they can make a positive difference.

CHAPTER 6

Encouraging Curiosity

"I think, at a child's birth, if a mother could ask a fairy godmother to endow it with the most useful gift, that gift would be curiosity."
—Eleanor Roosevelt[57]

Curiosity promotes a thirst for knowledge and exploration, empowering children to become active learners, critical thinkers, and problem solvers.

THE POWER OF CURIOSITY IN THE LIVES OF NASA TRAILBLAZERS KATHERINE JOHNSON, DOROTHY VAUGHAN, AND MARY JACKSON

The stories of Katherine Johnson, Dorothy Vaughan, and Mary Jackson testify to the transformative power of curiosity and perseverance. These three African American women significantly contributed to NASA when racial and gender barriers were formidable. Their pioneering efforts were instrumental in advancing NASA's missions and have left an indelible mark on science, technology, engineering, and mathematics (STEM).

---

57 Eleanor Roosevelt, "Curiosity Quotes," Goodreads, https://www.goodreads.com/quotes/tag/curiosity, accessed May 16, 2024.

Katherine Johnson: A Curiosity for Numbers

Katherine Johnson's journey began with an early fascination with numbers. Her exceptional talent for mathematics became evident at a young age, and she pursued this passion with unwavering determination. Johnson's relentless curiosity and analytical prowess at NASA enabled her to perform complex calculations critical to the success of the first American spaceflights. Her calculations were so precise that astronaut John Glenn specifically requested her verification for his orbital mission, signifying the immense trust placed in her abilities. Johnson's contributions ensured the safety and success of numerous missions and paved the way for women and people of color in STEM fields.

Dorothy Vaughan: Mastering Emerging Technologies

Dorothy Vaughan's career at NASA was marked by her adaptability and keen interest in emerging technologies. Vaughan began working as a human computer, performing complex calculations manually. Her curiosity drove her to learn about the newly emerging field of electronic computing. She mastered the programming language FORTRAN, becoming an expert in computer programming and leading the West Area Computing unit. Vaughan's ability to foresee the importance of electronic computers and her dedication to mastering this technology ensured that her team remained integral to NASA's success during the space race. Her leadership and foresight were instrumental in breaking down racial and gender barriers within the organization.

Mary Jackson: Pursuing Engineering Challenges

Mary Jackson's journey at NASA was defined by her relentless curiosity and drive to tackle engineering challenges. She began her career working with engineer Kazimierz Czarnecki, where her hands-on experience fueled her desire to become an engineer. Jackson's determination led her to complete a training program that enabled her to become NASA's first black female engineer in 1958. Throughout her career, she faced and overcame significant barriers, advocating tirelessly for the professional advancement of women at NASA. In 1979, she transitioned to a role as Langley's Federal Women's Program Manager, focusing on improving opportunities for all women in the organization. Jackson's dedication to breaking down barriers and advocating for equality left a lasting legacy.

Katherine Johnson, Dorothy Vaughan, and Mary Jackson's successes at NASA were driven by their relentless curiosity and dedication to their work. Johnson's early fascination with numbers, Vaughan's commitment to mastering emerging computing technologies, and Jackson's pursuit of engineering challenges exemplify how curiosity can lead to groundbreaking achievements. Their stories highlight the importance of nurturing inquisitiveness and determination, proving that these qualities can propel individuals to overcome obstacles and achieve extraordinary success. Their legacies continue to inspire future generations of scientists, engineers, and mathematicians.

The book and film *Hidden Figures* played a pivotal role in bringing their stories to light, showcasing their contributions, and encouraging young women and people of color to pursue careers in STEM fields. Their achievements remind us that curiosity and resilience can transform the world.[58][59]

58 "Hidden Figures," Astrobites, April 27, 2020, https://astrobites.org/2020/04/27/hidden-figures/, accessed July 2, 2024.

59 "Women Who Achieve: NASA Trailblazers Katherine Johnson, Dorothy Vaughan, and Mary Jackson." *Pioneers in Precision Medicine and Health Security*, https://ppimhs.org/newspost/women-who-achieve-nasa-trailblazers-katherine-johnson-dorothy-vaughan-and-mary-jackson/#:~:text=This%20week%20we%20are%20shining,astronaut%20into%20orbit%2C%20John%20Glenn, accessed July 2, 2024.

A MASTER CLASS ON CURIOSITY FROM TED LASSO

Fostering curiosity is a cornerstone in unlocking your child's limitless potential. To illustrate this vital attribute, let's draw inspiration from a poignant scene in the acclaimed series *Ted Lasso*. In this "darts scene" (2020), Ted Lasso, the ever-optimistic coach, challenges an antagonist to a game of darts. What unfolds is a masterclass in the power of curiosity, underscoring its importance for children and everyone.

> Guys have underestimated me my entire life. And for years, I never understood why. It used to really bother me. But then one day, I was driving my little boy to school, and I saw this quote by Walt Whitman. It was painted on the wall there and said, "Be curious, not judgmental." I like that.
>
> So I get back in my car, and I'm driving to work, and all of a sudden it hits me. All them fellas that used to belittle me, not a single one of them were curious. You know, they thought they had everything all figured out, and so they judged everything and they judged everyone.
>
> And I realized that their underestimating me—who I was—had nothing to do with it. Because if they were curious, they would have asked questions. Questions like, "Have you played a lot of darts, Ted?" which I would have answered, "Yes, sir. Every Sunday afternoon at a sports bar with my father from age ten until I was sixteen when he passed away."[60]

In this moment, Ted reveals a profound truth: Curiosity can change perceptions and open doors to deeper understanding. We equip our children with a powerful tool when we encourage them to be curious. Curiosity fosters a mindset of exploration and growth. It prompts them to ask questions, seek new experiences, and embrace learning as a lifelong journey.

---

60 *"Ted Lasso* (2020) - Darts Scene," TheBestMovieClipsOnTheInternet, https://www. youtube.com/watch?v=3S16b-x5mRA&t=8s, accessed May 20, 2024.

NURTURING CURIOSITY: GREENFIELD
UNION SCHOOL DISTRICT'S LEGO PLAN

This excerpt is adapted from my book, *Every Student Deserves a Gifted Education*.[61]

Greenfield Union School District, under the dynamic leadership of Superintendent Zandra Jo Galván, has embarked on a transformative journey to foster curiosity and unlock every student's limitless potential. At the heart of this educational revolution is the district's adoption of the LEGO plan, a strategic partnership with LEGO Education. This initiative is designed to nurture curiosity, flexible thinking, and problem-solving skills among students, providing them with hands-on, experiential learning opportunities.

The LEGO plan is pivotal in sparking curiosity by encouraging students to engage in creative problem-solving and critical thinking. By participating in the FIRST LEGO League, students from Pre-K to sixth grade immerse themselves in STEM activities that require them to think on their feet, adapt to new challenges, and collaborate with their peers. These experiences are not only about building with LEGO bricks but also about constructing knowledge and developing a mindset that embraces flexibility and innovation.

Greenfield Union's curriculum integrates curiosity-driven education through interactive projects and real-world applications. This approach ensures that learning is relevant and engaging, allowing students to explore subjects that interest them deeply. The emphasis on curiosity as a guiding principle helps students develop a love for learning that goes beyond the classroom.

A significant aspect of Greenfield Union's success is its collaborative ethos. Educators, students, and families work together to create

---

61 Brian Butler, *Every Student Deserves a Gifted Education*, The Answer's In The Room Press, 2023.

an environment where curiosity and flexible thinking thrive. Open dialogue and idea-sharing are encouraged, fostering a community that values questions and sees them as the seeds of innovation.

In the nurturing environment of Greenfield Union School District, curiosity is more than an educational goal—it is integral to the district's identity. Superintendent Galván's visionary leadership and the transformative LEGO partnership have created a vibrant community where students are empowered to explore, question, and realize their limitless potential. This journey of nurturing curiosity stands as an inspiring model for other educational institutions.

Why Curiosity Matters

Curiosity is more than just a desire to know more. It's an attitude of openness and wonder. It helps children:

Build empathy: Children become more empathetic and understanding by asking questions and learning about others' experiences.

Enhance problem-solving skills: Curious minds are adept at exploring different solutions and thinking creatively.

Develop resilience: Curiosity drives a love for learning, which in turn fosters resilience in the face of challenges and failures.

By instilling the value of curiosity, we set children on a lifelong learning and discovery path. Just as Ted Lasso realized the transformative power of curiosity, we too can unlock the limitless potential within our children by encouraging their natural inquisitiveness. Let us embrace and champion curiosity as a fundamental attribute, paving the way for our children to explore, grow, and thrive.

Providing Other Opportunities/Experiences for Parents to Teach Curiosity

Science Clubs or Camps: Science education can incorporate cultural perspectives by exploring scientific contributions from diverse cultures.

Nature Exploration: Nature exploration can include learning about traditional ecological knowledge from different cultural groups and fostering curiosity and respect for diverse ways of understanding and interacting with the natural world.

Reflection Questions for Parents

1. How do you think curiosity impacts a child's development, based on your own experiences or observations?

2. Reflect on a time when curiosity led to a significant learning moment or breakthrough in your life or the life of someone you know.

3. Consider the role of empathy in fostering curiosity. How can encouraging curiosity enhance a child's ability to understand and relate to others?

4. How does Ted Lasso's story illustrate the transformative power of curiosity? What lessons can we learn from his experience?

5. Think about a challenge or problem you've faced recently. How might a curious mindset have influenced your approach to solving it?

6. How can parents cultivate an environment that nurtures and supports their child's natural curiosity?

What Parents Can Do Today

1. Model Curiosity: Demonstrate your curiosity by asking questions and seeking new knowledge. Let your child see you engaged in learning and discovery.

2. Create a Curious Environment: Provide books, educational games, and opportunities for exploration. Encourage activities that stimulate their imagination and intellect.

3. Encourage Questions: Welcome your child's questions and take the time to explore answers together. Celebrate their inquisitiveness.

4. Expose Them to New Experiences: Introduce your child to diverse cultures, ideas, and environments. Travel, visit museums, and participate in community events to broaden their horizons.

5. Be Patient and Supportive: Foster a safe space for your child to express curiosity without fear of judgment or criticism. Support their interests, even if they differ from your own.

CHAPTER 7

Embracing Flexible Thinking

"The measure of intelligence is the ability to change."
—Albert Einstein[62]

Flexible thinking enables children to adapt their approaches when faced with new challenges, fostering mental resilience.

DON'T GIVE UP ON THE FIRST EPISODE!
A LESSON FROM THE KITCHEN

I'm not a big television watcher, but sometimes Kathleen and I sit together and a series catches our interest. One evening, as Kathleen was flipping through channels, she started a series she had already watched during her bout with COVID while being quarantined. Despite her familiarity with the show, we began watching it together. I found the first episode somewhat confusing, but I decided to continue watching, encouraged by Kathleen.

The episode that truly captured my attention involves the restaurant crew facing a significant problem. The series revolves around a diverse group of individuals working in a family restaurant, which a brother has returned to save. In this episode, a crucial piece of kitchen equipment breaks down right before opening time, rendering the oven and refrigerator unusable.

---

62 Albert Einstein, "Flexibility Quotes," Goodreads, https://www.goodreads.com/quotes/tag/flexibility, accessed May 27, 2024.

The crew has to think quickly and work together. They use an unoccupied building next door, setting up a makeshift grill outside. They also use ice from the freezer to keep food cool and switch to cash-only payments since the credit card system is down. This scenario requires the team to think flexibly, communicate precisely, and maintain self-control despite the stress. Their collective effort and optimism helped them avoid closing the restaurant for the day.

This story illustrates the importance of flexible thinking and problem-solving. The team has to adapt to unexpected challenges and find creative solutions. This is what we want for our children—to be able to change gears, adapt, and avoid getting stuck in one way of doing things when circumstances change.

It is crucial to teach and model flexible thinking to our children. These attributes are not innate; they must be taught, learned, modeled, and reinforced. By helping our kids develop flexible thinking and problem-solving skills, we prepare them to handle various challenges throughout their lives, no matter their path or the obstacles they face.

WHAT FLEXIBLE THINKING COULD LOOK LIKE AT HOME USING LEGOS

Mia's passion for LEGO building wasn't just a hobby; it was a way for her to express her creativity and explore her problem-solving skills. As she continued to build her bridge, she encountered another challenge. The design she had in mind required intricate detailing, but she couldn't find the specific pieces she needed.

Rather than feeling frustrated, Mia saw this as an opportunity to think outside the box. She rummaged through her LEGO collection, examining each piece with a new perspective. Suddenly, she spotted a set of small gears and wheels tucked away in a corner. With a spark of inspiration, she realized she could use them to add intricate texture and depth to her bridge.

Excited by her discovery, Mia eagerly incorporated the gears and wheels into her design. As she experimented with different placements and configurations, her bridge began to take on a whole new dimension. What was once a simple structure now boasted intricate patterns and dynamic movement, thanks to Mia's flexible thinking.

Her parents watched in amazement as Mia transformed her initial idea into something beyond their expectations. They marveled at her ingenuity and resourcefulness, realizing that flexible thinking wasn't just about overcoming obstacles—it was about embracing new possibilities and pushing the boundaries of creativity.

Encouraged by her success, Mia continued to explore the endless possibilities of LEGO building, each project sparking new challenges and opportunities for innovation. With each creation, she honed her skills in flexible thinking, proving that with a little imagination, there's no limit to what you can achieve, even within the confines of a basic LEGO set.

Providing Other Opportunities/Experiences for Parents to Teach Flexible Thinking

Chess Club: Enroll your child in a chess club. Chess encourages strategic thinking and requires players to adapt their strategies based on their opponent's moves. It's an inclusive activity enjoyed globally, teaching children to appreciate different perspectives and tactics.

Robotics Clubs: Join a robotics club where children can explore innovations and applications of technology from different cultures. This encourages flexible thinking and creativity as children learn to solve problems in multiple ways and understand diverse approaches to technology.

P.S. Chess or robotics club: Your child's school or the local Boys and Girls Club may offer free or low-cost options, as well as their school or other local organizations.

Reflection Questions for Parents

1. Reflecting on Challenges:

Think about a recent challenge your child faced. How did they approach it? Did they stick to one solution, or did they try different methods?

How do you handle changes or unexpected situations? What might your reactions teach your child about flexibility?

2. Encouraging Diverse Problem-Solving:

Can you recall when your child came up with a unique solution to a problem? How did you respond?

How can you model flexible thinking in your everyday life?

3. Understanding the Value of Flexibility:

Why do you think flexible thinking is important for your child's development?

How do you discuss the importance of being adaptable with your child?

4. Evaluating Opportunities:

What activities or clubs is your child currently involved in? How do these activities promote or hinder flexible thinking?

How can you introduce more activities that encourage flexible thinking and problem-solving?

What Parents Can Do Today

1. Model Flexible Thinking: Share personal stories about when you had to change your approach to solve a problem. Use phrases like "Let's think of another way to solve this" or "How else can we look at this situation?" when helping your child with a problem.

2. Encourage Diverse Experiences: Enroll your child in activities like chess or robotics clubs, which naturally promote strategic thinking and adaptability. Expose your child to different cultures through books, movies, and food to broaden their perspectives.

3. Create a Problem-Solving Environment: When a problem arises, encourage brainstorming sessions where every idea is considered. Celebrate creative and unconventional solutions, even if they don't work out, to show that trying different approaches is valuable.

4. Support Through Challenges: When your child encounters a difficult situation, guide them to think about various solutions rather than providing an immediate answer. Discuss past challenges and reflect on how different strategies led to different outcomes.

Integrating these reflection questions and activities into your daily routine can help your child develop the flexible thinking skills necessary for adapting to an ever-changing world.

CHAPTER 8

Cultivating Optimism

"Every problem has a gift for you in its hands."
—Richard Bach[63]

Optimism shapes children's outlook on life, empowering them to see opportunities in setbacks, maintain hope in adversity, and approach challenges with determination. While all 7 Essential Attributes are important, it's crucial to recognize that growth in these areas is a continuous journey, even for adults.

THE LITTLE ENGINE THAT COULD

Many of us have read the timeless classic *The Little Engine That Could*, which demonstrated the ultimate example of an optimistic spirit. In the book by Watty Piper, a small engine is faced with the daunting task of pulling a long train over a high mountain after larger locomotives refuse. Despite the challenges, the little engine bravely accepts the responsibility, repeating the mantra "I think I can" as it conquers the obstacle. The tale teaches valuable lessons about determination, perseverance, and self-belief, resonating with readers of all ages.[64]

63 Richard Bach, Inspire My Kids, https://inspiremykids.com/great-quotes-for-kids-about-optimism-and-positive-thinking/, accessed May 16, 2024.
64 Watty Piper, *The Little Engine That Could*, Philomel Books, 2005.

THE POWER OF OPTIMISM:
LESSONS FROM THE GOLF COURSE

The saying "Golf is a good walk spoiled" has been attributed to several sources, including Mark Twain and William Gladstone.[65]

Regardless of its origin, the sentiment resonates with many golf enthusiasts. Like life, golf is full of challenges that require a positive outlook and resilience.

Golf, as an individual sport, offers unique lessons in character development. It teaches optimism, self-control, perseverance, empathy, curiosity, flexible thinking, and precise communication, which are vital for personal growth, especially for children.

Golf mirrors life's ups and downs, demanding optimism almost minute by minute. Players face bad shots, tough lies/position of the ball on the ground, and difficult courses, forcing them to maintain a positive attitude. Despite these challenges, the beauty of the course and the joy of being outdoors often outweigh the game's frustrations.

Recently, I played a round of golf with my friend Mark. It was a beautiful day with clear skies and 80-degree weather. However, my game was far from perfect. My shots were erratic, and I struggled throughout most of the round. Despite this, the experience remained enjoyable because of the scenic walk and pleasant company.

As we finished the final hole, we noticed a man preparing to play the next course. Remarkably, he was about to play from a wheelchair, ready to take on the same challenges we faced. His determination and optimism were inspiring, far exceeding the resilience we needed to muster during our game.

This encounter underscored the importance of maintaining a positive mindset, no matter the difficulty. The man in the wheelchair

---

65 "Golf Is a Good Walk Spoiled," Quote Investigator, https://quoteinvestigator. com/2010/05/28/golf-good-walk/, accessed May 20, 2024.

exemplified the virtues of persistence, optimism, and flexible thinking. His ability to embrace the challenge of golf from a wheelchair highlighted the strength of character that individual sports can foster.

Golf teaches us the value of optimism, perseverance, and finding joy in the journey. The story of the man in the wheelchair reminds us that with the right attitude, any challenge can become an opportunity for growth.

FIX YOUR FACE! RACHEL SCOTT'S JOURNEY TO SUCCESS—FROM DISAPPOINTMENT TO OPTIMISM

In her commencement speech (2024) at the University of Southern California, Rachel Scott, senior congressional correspondent for ABC, shared her journey of overcoming failure. She recounted how, eleven years earlier, she was rejected from USC, her dream school, not once but twice. Despite feeling devastated and ashamed, her mother's advice to "fix your face" encouraged her to shift her perspective and move forward.

Determined to succeed, Scott focused on academics, secured top grades, and applied for numerous internships. Her efforts paid off when, at nineteen, she became one of the youngest interns at the White House. This experience ignited her passion for political journalism. When she eventually transferred to USC, she realized the initial rejection guided her toward greater opportunities.

Scott emphasized embracing failure and rejection for their ability to redirect us toward unexpected blessings and new paths. She urged the graduates to be grateful for the lessons learned from setbacks and never underestimate the power of their stories.[66]

---

66 "Rachel Scott on the Power of Failure - USC Commencement," YouTube, https://www.youtube.com/watch?v=5AlTNcMNhAw, accessed June 27, 2024.

THE BENEFITS OF TEAM SPORTS

My parents allowed me to play team sports as early as I can remember, beginning at around five years old. I continued through high school and college and became a professional athlete. I was taught the value of optimism by participating in team sports. Playing team sports, particularly basketball, taught me the importance of believing in myself even when I wasn't successful. As a three-point shooting specialist in college, I knew that making four out of ten shots was considered very good. This meant I had to remain optimistic despite missing six out of ten shots, more than I made. This principle applies to other sports as well. For instance, in baseball and fast-pitch softball, a .300 batting average is considered good, but it also means failing 70 percent of the time.

Team sports promote optimism by fostering teamwork, resilience, and a positive mindset, regardless of cultural background. Playing team sports often meant I was teammates with people from all backgrounds. Getting to know each other promotes inclusivity and understanding.

In the May 2024 issue of *Costco Connection,* Andrea Downing Peck's article "Come Together: Benefits of Team Sports for Adults" discusses the advantages of team sports. In this article, an aside explores the benefits of team sports for children.[67] According to a 2019 University of British Columbia study, engaging in team sports at an early age offers more than just teaching sportsmanship. The study found that children who participated in sports in fourth grade were more likely to continue playing into early adolescence and experienced better mental health.

Dr. David Soma, a physician at Mayo Clinic in Minnesota, highlights additional benefits for sports-playing kids, including a higher

---

[67] Andrea Downing Peck, "Come Together: Benefits of Team Sports for Adults," *Costco Connection*, May 2024, pp. 32-33.

likelihood of high school graduation and college attendance, increased rates of physical activity in adulthood, and lower instances of drug and alcohol use and teen pregnancy.

Playing team sports, for me, felt like a microcosm of the world we live in, as I had to get along with others, bounce back from heart-break, take a back seat to teammates at times for the good of the team, and not always see eye-to-eye with coaches. I was constantly evaluated by people watching my practices and games, which taught me self-control and persistence. I learned to empathize with others who might be having a bad day or a prolonged period of not play-ing well (a slump). I learned to think flexibly and to change how I approached improving, even to the point of adapting within a split-second during games. I had to stay curious, continually learning different skills to get better.

If you think about it, I just revisited every one of the 7 Essential Attributes addressed in this book through sports.

Many other activities help teach optimism, but sports were a huge part of why I can do the things I do today, even if they are unrelated to sports. It's crucial to help children understand that optimism amid setbacks is a necessary part of the learning process. Embracing this perspective is essential for success in all aspects of life.

Providing Other Opportunities/Experiences or Parents to Teach Optimism

Outdoor Adventure Programs: Outdoor adventures can incorporate cultural elements such as traditional storytelling, music, or art, fos-tering optimism and appreciation for diverse cultural heritages while exploring nature.

Individual and Team Sports Participation: Individual and team sports, such as tennis, golf, track, swimming, soccer, basketball, or volleyball, to name a few, are wonderful vehicles to teach optimism. Through these experiences, children can learn the importance of a positive mindset, perseverance, and resilience. Reinforce optimism by celebrating effort over outcome, discussing how setbacks are growth opportunities, highlighting the importance of self-improvement in individual sports, and supporting teammates in team sports. This approach helps children develop a hopeful attitude and the confidence to face challenges in sports and life.

Arts and Creative Expression: Involve children in artistic activities such as painting, music, dance, theater, or writing. These forms of creative expression allow children to explore their emotions, develop a positive outlook, and see challenges as opportunities for growth. Reinforce optimism by celebrating the creative process rather than focusing solely on the final product, discussing how mistakes can lead to unexpected beauty, and encouraging persistence in mastering a skill. This approach helps children build confidence, embrace their unique talents, and maintain a hopeful perspective in their artistic endeavors and everyday life.

Reflection Questions for Parents

1. How has optimism influenced your life journey? Reflect on when maintaining a positive outlook helped you overcome a challenge or setback.

2. Consider the stories of *The Little Engine That Could* and the golfer in a wheelchair. How do these narratives illustrate the power of optimism and perseverance in the face of adversity?

3. Reflect on your experiences with individual or team sports or other group activities. How did participating in these activities shape your understanding of optimism, teamwork, and resilience?

4. How did encountering the golfer in a wheelchair impact your perception of optimism and resilience? Reflect on the lessons you learned from witnessing his determination and positive mindset.

5. Think about the role of optimism in fostering resilience and adaptability in children. How can parents encourage and cultivate an optimistic mindset in their children?

6. How do books and stories contribute to teaching children about optimism and resilience? Reflect on any stories or books from your childhood that had a similar impact on you.

What Parents Can Do Today

1. Model Optimism: Show a positive outlook in your own life, especially when facing challenges. Let your child witness your resilience and determination. Embrace Carol Dweck's "Power of Yet" philosophy from her growth mindset research. Remind your children that they may not have succeeded at something "YET," but with optimism and persistence, they can achieve success. Encourage them to view setbacks as temporary hurdles and chances for growth, instilling in them a belief in their capacity to learn and progress over time.

2. Encourage Positive Self-Talk: Teach your child the power of positive self-talk by using phrases like "I can" and "I will" when facing challenges. Encourage them to reframe negative thoughts into positive ones.

3. Celebrate Effort and Progress: Focus on effort rather than just outcomes. Celebrate your child's efforts and progress, emphasizing the importance of perseverance and resilience.

4. Promote Gratitude: Encourage your child to cultivate gratitude by journaling or sharing daily gratitude around mealtime. Focusing on the positives can help foster an optimistic mindset.

5. Provide Diverse Experiences: Expose your child to various activities, including team sports, outdoor adventures, and cultural experiences. These experiences can teach resilience, teamwork, and optimism in different contexts.

Numerous other books also teach these valuable lessons to young readers. For instance, *Oh, the Places You'll Go!* (1990)[68] by Dr. Seuss encourages children to embrace life's adventures and overcome challenges confidently. Additionally, *The Dot* (2004) by Peter H. Reynolds[69] inspires creativity and self-expression by illustrating the power of believing in oneself. For older readers, *Wonder* (2012) by R. J. Palacio[70] portrays the importance of kindness and acceptance in the face of adversity. These stories, among others, are powerful tools for nurturing an optimistic outlook and building resilience in children and adolescents.

UNITING ALL 7 ATTRIBUTES

An Example of How the 7 Essential Attributes Were Used in Demolishing and Building a Driveway

The professionals who demolished and rebuilt our driveway epitomize sharing their gifts with the world. Effective work requires high physical, cognitive, and emotional intelligence.

Demolishing and rebuilding a concrete driveway requires physical skills like strength, coordination, and spatial awareness to operate machinery and handle materials. Cognitive skills such as problem-solving are essential to overcome challenges during demolition and

---

68 Dr. Seuss, *Oh, the Places You'll Go!*, Random House, 1990.
69 Peter H. Reynolds, *The Dot*, Weston Woods Studio, 2004.
70 R. J. Palacio, *Wonder*, Alfred A. Knopf, 2012.

construction, while effective communication is crucial for coordinating with team members. Perseverance is needed to see the project through to completion despite obstacles. Specific mathematical knowledge is also required, including geometry for measuring angles and distances, algebra for calculating material quantities and costs, and trigonometry to calculate the slope or incline of the driveway for proper drainage based on its length and height. Additionally, basic arithmetic skills are essential for accurate measurements and calculations throughout the project.

Let's put it all together by using the building the driveway example to illustrate how each of the 7 Essential Attributes in their designated chapters is used during the process. This example can be translated into most professions or endeavors.

Chapter 2: Fostering Persistence

Just as the driveway professionals showed perseverance in completing their tasks despite various challenges, teaching our children the value of persistence helps them tackle complex subjects and projects. Encouraging them to keep trying even when things get tough will instill a can-do attitude.

Chapter 3: Nurturing Precise Communication

Effective communication is critical in coordinating complex tasks, as demonstrated by the driveway team. By nurturing precise communication skills in our children, we help them express their thoughts clearly and work collaboratively with others, whether in school or the future in the way that driveway team demonstrated.

Chapter 4: Developing Self-control

Self-control is necessary for managing the physical demands and precision required in construction work. Similarly, helping children develop self-control will enable them to manage their emotions, focus on their studies, and achieve their goals without distractions.

Chapter 5: Building Empathy

The teamwork seen in the driveway project also involves empathy—understanding and addressing the needs of others. Building empathy in our children will help them form strong, supportive relationships and work effectively in diverse environments.

Chapter 6: Encouraging Curiosity

The problem-solving aspect of construction requires a curious mind eager to find solutions. Encouraging curiosity in children will inspire them to explore, ask questions, and seek knowledge, driving their desire to learn and innovate.

Chapter 7: Embracing Flexible Thinking

Challenges in construction often require flexible thinking and adapting to new situations. By teaching children to embrace flexible thinking, we prepare them to approach problems with creativity and adaptability, essential skills in our ever-changing world.

Chapter 8: Cultivating Optimism

Finally, optimism helps professionals see projects through to completion despite obstacles. Cultivating optimism in our children will empower them to stay positive and resilient, even when faced with setbacks, ensuring they remain motivated and confident in their abilities.

My Plea! Redefining Professionalism
and Celebrating All Paths to Excellence

I just wanted to extend a personal plea! Let's celebrate all forms of professionalism, recognizing that each path to excellence is valuable and worthy of respect. Let's stop with the blue-collar and white-collar labels! It should be about professionalism and dedication to excelling at what one does.

In the book *Collaboration for Career and Technical Education*, 2020, Paul Farmer and Wendy Constable write about career and technical education misconceptions. They say, regrettably, there are still schools where career and technical education (CTE) is considered a place to send students to increase their GPAs because the work is supposedly easy. Other schools see their CTE programs as a place to send students struggling in other courses. Buffum et al. (2018) state that many schools currently remove students from college prep coursework and place them into vocational tracks because they deem the students incapable of succeeding on the college prep track. Vocational pathways can be outstanding pathways to post-secondary education. Still, students should leave high school with the academic skills and behaviors necessary to succeed in university and vocational settings.[71]

It's time we stop viewing CTE classes and careers as a second-tier option in education and society. The American College Test (ACT), 2006 conducted a study that found students aspiring to be electricians, plumbers, carpenters, and upholsterers need the same literacy and mathematics skills as at least first-year college students.[72] An independent plumber, for instance, needs to set up their business, manage finances, communicate effectively with clients, perhaps start and run

---

71 Paul Farmer and Wendy Constable, *Collaboration for Career and Technical Education*, Solution Tree Press, 2020.
72 ACT, Inc., *Ready for College and Ready for Work: Same or Different?*, 2006.

their own website, have a social media presence, etc. The better they are at running their own business—and the more professional they seem in clients' eyes—the greater their income will be. They could perhaps run the business into their sixties or seventies, hiring workers to do the plumbing jobs instead of solely relying on their manual labor, which might wear out their bodies by their fifties.

We should prepare all students as if they are going to college—not because every student needs to attend college, but because they all need strong literacy and numeracy skills and must embrace the idea that learning is a skill for life in any field of their choosing. Just try taking a test to become an electrician or carpenter; high literacy and numeracy are crucial.

Let's move beyond the labels of white-collar and blue-collar. Why do we continue to sort and select careers as if one is inherently better than the other? All paths should be respected and valued equally.

As we move forward, hearing from those who have lived these principles is essential. In the upcoming chapter, *Hopes and Dreams*, we'll delve into real-life stories and experiences from parents that will provide inspiration and practical insights for teaching, modeling, and fostering these essential qualities in your children.

I will again emphasize that by fostering these seven attributes in our children, we can help them develop the skills and mindset needed to excel in any path they choose.

CHAPTER 9

Hopes and Dreams

This chapter concludes the book perfectly by encapsulating the essence of parental aspirations and the collective wisdom of the parents who contributed their stories. It celebrates the shared parenting experience and is a testament to the hopes and dreams of parents that every child can realize their limitless future through love, support, and access to opportunities.

In this chapter, I aim to explore the diverse spectrum of parenting situations and family dynamics. I hope readers resonate with one or more of the stories shared here. Encountering family experiences that closely or somewhat mirror ours fosters a connection and offers valuable learning opportunities.

To protect confidentiality, I have changed names and locations and added other details in some of the stories generated from the parent questionnaires. Juana Tlatelpa is the only story in which I use the real names of those written about.

While we can glean insights from families whose experiences differ from ours, there's a unique comfort in learning from those who share a similar background and family dynamic or face similar challenges. Therefore, you'll encounter families from various walks of life—adoptive parents, birth parents, and others—united by their hopes and dreams for their children.

Parents have dreams for their children's future from the moment they are born or whenever they come into their care. These dreams often evolve, influenced by the child's growing interests and the experiences shaping their development. In this chapter, parents recount their initial hopes and how these aspirations have transformed over time, providing a glimpse into the dynamic nature of parenting.

I chose this first story to underscore the universal themes of providing access to opportunities that drive every parent's dream of helping their child find the "song within them."

FROM LITTLE LEAGUE REJECT TO MLB STAR: A MOTHER CREATING ACCESS TO OPPORTUNITIES

Mookie Betts' journey to becoming one of Major League Baseball's top players is a testament to the power of parental support and determination. When Mookie was just five years old, his mother, Diana Collins, took him to sign up for Little League baseball. However, they faced an unexpected obstacle: every coach they approached turned Mookie away, deeming him too small to play for their teams. One coach even told Mookie's mom that he preferred larger, more athletic players.

Mookie was heartbroken, telling his mother with tears streaming down his face, "I'm not going to be able to play." But Diana refused to let these rejections stop her son from playing the game he loved. Instead of accepting defeat, she decided to take matters into her own hands. Diana formed her own team, gathering a group of misfit players who had also been overlooked by other teams.

Although Mookie's team won only one game that season, that lone victory was particularly sweet—it came against the coach who had initially rejected Mookie. Despite the obstacles, Diana's determination to create opportunities for her son allowed Mookie to showcase his talent and develop his skills. Her coaching approach emphasized not just playing the game but playing to win. She would tell Mookie during that game against the coach who rejected him, "Every ball that comes, I want you to get it. I don't care where the ball is." This relentless drive to succeed and prove his worth became a defining characteristic of Mookie's playing style.

Today, Mookie Betts is a seven-time All-Star and two-time World Series champion. His journey from a little boy told he was too small to play to become one of the highest-paid players in Major League Baseball underscores the vital role parents can play in supporting and nurturing their children's talents. Diana Collins' unwavering support and resourcefulness ensured that Mookie had the opportunity to pursue his passion, ultimately leading him to greatness.[73] [74] [75]

THE TLATELPA FAMILY BLUEPRINT: RAISING CHILDREN WITH CONFIDENCE, INDEPENDENCE, AND HEART

I enjoyed working with Juana Tlatelpa at Mount Eagle Elementary School. Through our interactions, I quickly recognized Juana as an incredible parent, deeply committed to her children's growth and success. I invited her to share her journey of raising her children— Stephany, Janeth, and Emily—for the final chapter of my book. Here is Juana's story in her own words:

> When I had my twin daughters, Stephany and Janeth, my primary hopes and dreams were for them to be healthy and reach their developmental milestones. Their premature birth, each weighing

73 "How 5-Year-Old Mookie Betts Got Revenge on the Baseball Field, Reddit, https://www.reddit.com/r/baseball/comments/jr89om/how_5yearold_mookie_betts_got_revenge_on_the/?rdt=56373, accessed June 17, 2024.
74 Instagram post, https://www.instagram.com/p/C7r2-6SiKyc/?igsh=MXcyOHUza-GRhODZwYw%3D%3D&img_index=1, accessed June 17, 2024.
75 "Mookie Betts," YouTube, https://www.youtube.com/shorts/puwn6ZG8duI, accessed July 10, 2024.

only four pounds, made me especially conscious of their health and growth. As they grew older, my dreams evolved. I wanted them to achieve their highest potential and develop their unique identities, as they were shy and initially only played with each other. Stephany struggled academically compared to Janeth, so I ensured she received the tutoring she needed and encouraged Janeth to help her sister whenever possible.

When Emily was born fourteen years later, I felt more mature as a parent. My hopes for her were similar—health and independence—but I also faced challenges as she had a speech impairment. I immediately sought help from her pediatrician and worked diligently to support her speech development. By the time my twin daughters reached high school, my husband and I had instilled in them the values of responsibility, hard work, respect, and goal orientation, leading them to attend George Mason University. Both hold master's degrees in Curriculum and Instruction and are elementary school teachers. Inspired by her sisters, Emily is following in their footsteps and is currently a junior at George Mason University, aiming to become an elementary school teacher.

All three of my children were raised in a family-oriented home where dinner time was sacred. We would eat together and discuss our day, fostering a sense of responsibility and organization as they knew homework time followed dinner. They were involved in various after-school activities like swimming, ballet, dance, and karate, which kept them busy and taught them how to balance their time. We enjoyed family trips to the beach, zoos and museums and occasional Disney World visits. As the twins grew older, they started participating in more sophisticated experiences with Emily, such as attending concerts and theater plays. These activities helped them develop confidence and trust in us as parents. Even now, as adults, we cherish our time together, whether shopping at the mall or simply enjoying each other's company.

Playtime was a crucial way we encouraged our children to explore different interests. The twins enjoyed pretending to be various professionals, from teachers to grocery workers, which allowed them to explore different careers through play. Emily followed suit, often imitating her sisters by pretending to be a college student or a teacher. The safe environment provided by Mount Eagle Elementary School and the community support from my part-time job as a property manager also played significant roles in their development. When my twins showed a keen interest in reading, particularly Judy Blume books, I took them to the library regularly and bought them books from their favorite series. They also enjoyed collecting stationery items, so we visited the Dollar Tree Store monthly. Emily, on the other hand, loved arts and crafts. We frequently visited Michaels to buy her supplies for her creative projects.

While my husband and I were initially overprotective of our twins, Emily experienced more independence early on. She attended childcare at just four months old and developed skills that her sisters hadn't at her age. We supported their decisions about after-school activities and valued their choices, such as when the twins decided to stop after-school activities in fifth grade or when Emily chose to stop swimming classes in third grade. When my twins faced challenges in math, a coworker's daughter, who was in college, volunteered to tutor them, boosting their confidence. Emily, who struggled with dyslexia and speech delays, received support from knowledgeable colleagues and an understanding of the research, which helped her succeed academically. Through these experiences, all my daughters learned the importance of persistence, self-control, and empathy.

We always emphasized the importance of diverse experiences to help our children develop appreciation and respect for different cultures. This exposure has been instrumental in their careers as educators. My twins, now teachers, continue to instill these values in their students. Each of my daughters brings unique gifts to our family. Emily is the charming, loving, and caring one who uplifts everyone. Janeth loves discovering and cooking new Mexican recipes, while Stephany is passionate about organization, ensuring our home stays tidy and functional.

We've always strived to balance our hopes for our children with their unique needs and learning preferences. My husband and I learned not to pressure Emily to keep up with her sisters but to support her in achieving her goals at her own pace. We encourage open communication, especially during family dinners, which helps us understand and nurture their interests.[76]

The Tlatelpa family's story is a testament to the power of dedicated parenting, community support, and the importance of nurturing each child's unique path. Their journey reflects many of the key principles of this book, emphasizing the significance of fostering confidence, resilience, and a growth mindset in children.

DISCOVERING UNIQUENESS IN A DIVERSE FAMILY

A former colleague and friend of mine courageously and honestly shared his story as a same-sex couple and their journey into parenthood through adoption. Their son's arrival marked the beginning of a challenging yet hopeful chapter. As foster-to-adopt parents, they were faced with navigating their son's early academic struggles against the backdrop of past traumas.

---

76 Juana Tlatelpa, personal communication, June 2024.

They adopted him when he was in elementary school, and he had been in multiple foster homes after having been taken from his birth mother. They were unsure of the extent to which these deeply distressing and disturbing experiences were having on their adoptive son. But they knew something had happened before they became his parents.

Their dreams for him were profound yet immediate: to heal from past wounds, unearth his passions, and help him discover the joy of learning. From the outset, his love for reading and sports shone through, but as he navigated the complexities of middle school, academic obstacles emerged, prompting evaluations for attention deficit hyperactive disorder and a concerted effort to address his trauma.

Their network, comprising friends, educators, and mental health providers, proved invaluable in giving him the support they needed when they as parents did not know what to do or when their son seemed more receptive to other adults, which isn't that unusual. Together, they offered guidance, encouragement, and at times mentorship.

Their journey was punctuated by deep introspection spurred by questions about family dynamics and learning. Reflecting on their son's unique gifts, they marveled at his charm and social ease, which endeared him to others effortlessly. His athletic prowess was equally remarkable, providing an avenue for him to excel and thrive.

Family dynamics played a pivotal role in shaping their son's development. Having lived with multiple foster families, he quickly adapted to new environments, learning to forge connections and find his place. Exposure to diverse opportunities broadened his horizons, igniting his aspirations and fueling his dreams.

Life was not without challenges, particularly in navigating societal expectations while fostering their son's individuality. Residing in an affluent community, they grappled with the pressure of academic excellence but prioritized their son's happiness and well-being above all else. This delicate balance underscored the importance of nurturing his unique talents amidst external pressures.

Their son's perception of his place within the family was shaped by his identity as a straight black boy with two white dads. While he thrived socially in elementary school, the middle school brought its share of identity struggles. High school ushered in the resurgence of the trauma he had faced before being adopted, which had to be continually addressed.

In the questionnaire, his parents emphasized the need for educators to approach each child with an open mind. They said that collaboration between parents and educators is critical to supporting children in schools.

After graduating from high school, their son enlisted in the military. For the parents, it was a moment filled with pride and uncertainty. Nevertheless, they stood by him steadfastly, supporting his decision with love and encouragement.

As their son embarked on his military career, their bond remained strong. His decision to serve his country stood as a testament to the values instilled in him by his adoptive parents—a legacy of resilience, courage, and unwavering determination.

As their son's story unfolds, the couple's hopes and dreams for him endure. From fostering confidence and resilience to nurturing his unique talents, they remain steadfast in their support, guiding him toward a future of endless possibilities. And as they watch him chart his course, their love remains a guiding light for him to continue to shine his gifts on the world.[77]

---

77 Anonymous, personal communication, June 2024 (a true story compiled via parent questionnaire).

HOPE FOR MY CHILDREN'S FUTURES: NURTURING KINDNESS, COMMUNITY, AND LIFELONG LEARNING

When my children were born, my main hope and dream was that they would be good humans. Of course, I wanted them to succeed in the important things, but above all, I just wanted them to be kind to everyone they met. As they have grown, I still want them to be good people. I don't believe in pushing my goals on them, and I want them to set out to achieve their hopes and dreams.

Both of my kids had different experiences from birth to kindergarten because of the opportunities where we lived when they were each at that stage. Also, Sam was in his prime early childhood during COVID-19, which influenced what we could offer him.

Lindsay's Story

From the beginning, Lindsay's path was marked by diverse experiences that shaped her early years. She started with a bilingual preschool and later attended a Spanish Montessori school, enriching her understanding of languages and cultures from an early age. Our community's offerings allowed her to explore activities like gymnastics, swim lessons, and art classes at the local community center. Trips to museums and even a visit to the Mexican Embassy broadened her horizons further.

Sporting events, from soccer to tee-ball and martial arts, became regular fixtures in Lindsay's schedule, fostering her physical development and social skills through team activities. Family time at the dinner table and cooking classes instilled a love for food and shared meals. Holidays and birthdays were celebrated with gusto, involving our entire circle of friends and family. Lindsay's educational journey was complemented by regular visits to the pediatrician and a rich assortment of books and activities, promoting both intellectual curiosity and emotional growth.

As she grew older, Lindsay's interests expanded to include outdoor adventures, science camps, and artistic pursuits like pottery and attending plays. She embraced learning through hands-on experiences, supported by activities like Kiwi Crate projects and frequent library visits. Our focus was on academics and nurturing her social connections and cultural awareness throughout her development.

Sam's Path

Sam's early years unfolded differently, shaped by his unique interests and our evolving family dynamics. His preschool days were part-time, allowing for a balance between structured learning and time at home. With my extended presence during his formative years, Sam thrived in environments like parent-child gymnastics and swim classes, where he could explore movement and water safety.

Like his sister, Sam's world expanded through travel and museum visits, providing him with firsthand experiences of history and science. Outdoor activities like gardening and regular family meals grounded him in practical skills and a connection to nature. Sporting events and playdates further enriched his social development, laying the groundwork for enduring friendships.

Our decision to move to Northern California brought new opportunities and challenges. While adjusting to rural life, we ensured Sam's involvement in community activities, including 4H programs and local events. These experiences built his sense of responsibility and community service and provided avenues for personal growth.

Like Lindsay, Sam's educational journey was supplemented by tailored interventions and activities that catered to his evolving interests. From homeschool lessons to engaging with educational platforms, we supported his explorations in technology and other subjects of intrigue. His participation in library programs, regular health check-ups, and seasonal traditions further enriched his childhood.

Navigating Choices and Challenges

Our parenting philosophy has always revolved around exposing our children to diverse opportunities and supporting their natural inclinations. We encouraged them to explore various activities—from sports to arts and beyond—allowing them to discover their passions independently. Lindsay, for instance, took the initiative to explore languages, arts, and mindfulness, reflecting her evolving interests and personal growth.

Balancing these opportunities with practical considerations like time management and financial constraints has been a constant challenge. Living in a rural setting necessitated careful planning, ensuring our children could access a broad spectrum of experiences despite geographic limitations. Our commitment to community involvement and leadership also played a crucial role, creating opportunities where none existed and fostering a sense of civic responsibility in Lindsay and Sam.

Looking ahead, our greatest aspiration remains unchanged: to raise children who are successful in their pursuits and compassionate contributors to society. We instill values of kindness, community support, and lifelong learning, believing these qualities will guide them toward fulfilling lives and meaningful contributions.[78]

---

78 Anonymous, personal communication, June 2024 (a true story compiled via parent questionnaire).

FOSTERING CONFIDENCE AND INDEPENDENCE: THE JOHNSON FAMILY'S JOURNEY OF PERSISTENCE, SELF-CONTROL, AND EMPATHY

When Sarah Johnson's daughters were born, her hopes were simple yet profound: She wished for them to grow up as good human beings— kind, thoughtful, and hard-working. As they grew, these hopes evolved into a more complex vision. Sarah and her husband began to joke that they just wanted their daughters to find fulfilling careers or to follow the path of Sarah's brother, who worked in "big law" for ten years, saved his earnings, and then pursued his passion for poetry—the practical way to pursue all dreams.

Raising two daughters with a neuropsychiatric disorder, Sarah's dreams took on a more immediate focus. One daughter struggled with emotional modulation, anger management, and reading people's intentions. The family's primary dream for her became helping her manage her condition so she could reconnect with herself.

From birth until kindergarten, the Johnson family ensured their daughters had rich and diverse experiences. These ranged from small, in-home daycare with nurturing providers to family dinners, in-home art projects, reading books, storytelling, and spending time with extended family. A standout influence was an amazing preschool teacher who ignited a passion for science in their oldest daughter. Additionally, activities like gymnastics and swim classes at the rec center, family trips, and play therapy for extreme anxiety starting at two years old were integral in their development.

Encouraging exploration of different interests, the Johnsons supported their daughters' endeavors even when met with resistance from extended family. For instance, Sarah had to have a serious conversation with her mother, who disapproved of her granddaughter's love for taekwondo. Despite these challenges, the family valued these activities for the life skills they imparted, such as perseverance, respect, and teamwork.

Their daughters' interests were met with encouragement and support. When their oldest daughter strongly desired to participate in taekwondo, the Johnsons allowed her to pursue it despite initial doubts. This decision proved beneficial, teaching her valuable lessons. Similarly, their youngest daughter's passion for horseback riding was nurtured, with the family making sacrifices to afford lessons that proved essential for her emotional regulation.

The Johnsons exposed their daughters to various hobbies, sports, arts, and academic subjects, always following their children's interests rather than imposing their expectations. They noticed a significant difference in social dynamics when they moved to rural Iowa, allowing for a more relaxed approach to their children's education and extracurricular activities. Their daughters had different schooling experiences—one in public school and the other homeschooled in a small, interest-led co-op run by Sarah.

As their daughters' interests evolved, the Johnsons encouraged them to persevere through challenging activities until a logical stopping point was reached. They supported quitting when necessary, emphasizing the importance of working hard at what they were passionate about and allowing space to explore new interests.

Balancing new opportunities with their daughters' independence, the Johnsons relied heavily on their support network. Like Sarah's mother-in-law, family members played crucial roles in helping with transportation and logistics, ensuring the children could participate in their chosen activities.

Throughout their journey, the Johnsons celebrated hard work and resilience rather than innate talent. They supported their daughters through challenges, fostering a growth mindset and celebrating effort over achievement. This approach aimed to teach their daughters valuable life skills, such as recovering from failure, identifying passions, and collaborating with others.

Sarah also emphasized the importance of educators and mentors recognizing and nurturing her daughters' strengths. While her oldest daughter benefited from supportive teachers who encouraged her creativity and intellectual growth, her youngest struggled to connect with teachers. This disparity highlighted the need for schools to support what Sarah termed "prickly" kids who may not easily connect but possess great potential.

One year at Pine Hill Elementary, Sarah observed the power of inclusive support through a drama club for children needing extra reading support. This club was not for students interested in drama but for those needing practice with decoding and fluency. It included kids who weren't always well-behaved or enthusiastic about school but thrived in this environment. Sarah saw firsthand the impact of giving children, who might otherwise be overlooked, the chance to shine. This experience underscored her belief that sometimes, the kids who push away the most are the ones who need the most support.

Ultimately, Sarah's hopes and dreams for all children center on their ability to follow their interests and have agency in their education. She advocates for a supportive environment where adults step back, allow children to lead, and act as guides. She believes in the transformative power of adults who see the potential in every child, providing the support needed for them to become brilliant and creative individuals.

In reflecting on the 7 Essential Attributes—persistence, precise communication, self-control, empathy, curiosity, flexible thinking, and optimism—Sarah notes these are ongoing journeys. Persistence, flexible thinking, and empathy are particularly emphasized for her family. Each family member contributes uniquely to this continuous growth, creating a nurturing environment where confidence and independence can flourish.[79]

THE AKAN FAMILY:
EMBRACING OPPORTUNITIES AND SEEING SUCCESS

When the Akan children were born, their parents' primary hopes and dreams were simple yet profound: for them to be happy and healthy. It was always important to the Akan family to support their kids' hopes and dreams, whatever those might be.

From birth until kindergarten, the Akan family provided their children with various experiences to help them develop socially, emotionally, and academically. They had dinner together as a family every night, went to church every Sunday, and enrolled in Sunday School starting at age two. They attended various Vacation Bible Schools to expose them to different environments and help them make friends. They took annual family trips in the summer so the children would have memorable experiences to share. They participated in summer reading clubs at the local library and bookstores, visited agricultural events at Mt. Vernon, and involved themselves in athletics, with their son starting soccer and their daughter starting dance at age five. At age four, they began tumbling classes at the dance studio where Mrs. Akan had trained. Additionally, they joined Jack and Jill of America, Inc., an organization dedicated to nurturing leadership among African American children.

They exposed them to the arts through musical instruments, visual arts, and performing arts to encourage their exploration of interests. They made annual trips to the Kennedy Center for performances and supported their involvement in school bands. Their son switched from

79 Anonymous, personal communication, June 2024 (a true story compiled via parent questionnaire).

soccer to football at age seven and played basketball in the winter, learning the importance of teamwork and time management. Their daughter continued with dance until middle school, when she switched to basketball. They both joined scouting organizations.

When their children showed interests or talents, they supported them wholeheartedly. After testing into their school's Gifted and Talented Program, their son also participated in programs at the Johns Hopkins Center for Talented Youth, where he developed a love for science and working with animals. His summer internship at the USDA and his job as a kennel assistant at a local veterinarian's office fueled his passion for veterinary medicine, leading him to pursue a career as a veterinarian. Mrs. Akan believes all students should be able to participate in these experiences, not just those who do well on the test that day.

They made sure to expose their children to various hobbies, sports, arts, and academic subjects with the support of their network of family, friends, schools, and community organizations. Their daughter loved to read and debate, which led her to join the mock trial team in high school. Watching her succeed in mock trials inspired her to pursue a degree in political science, followed by a JD in law school and an EdD. She is now a managing director of several school locations for a national academy.

As their children's interests evolved, the Akan family adapted their support. They balanced introducing new opportunities by allowing them independence and encouraging them to decide about their activities. They sought mentors and involved them in decision-making processes, fostering their growth and development. This adaptability reassured the children that their parents were always there to support them, no matter how their interests changed.

Exposure to diverse experiences was crucial in helping their children identify their strengths. The Akan family strongly believes in the importance of such exposure, as it broadens children's horizons and helps them discover their passions. Their support network facilitated this exposure, from allowing their son to take veterinary courses at another college to form a pre-veterinary medicine club with guest speakers and support from his college. Schools and organizations played a significant role by listening to students' needs and supporting their dreams.

Mrs. Akan's hopes and dreams for all children are to strive to remain lifelong learners and enjoy what they do. She wants them to know that their contributions improve the world. As parents, the Akan family believes they must nurture and support their children's hopes and dreams, teach them to seek opportunities, and help them understand how these opportunities can shape their future. Mrs. Akan believes everyone is unique and brings something valuable to the table; their role is to help them unleash their limitless potential.[80]

As we conclude this chapter, we are reminded that every parent's journey is a collection of hopes, dreams, and challenges. Through the stories shared here—from Mookie Betts' triumph over rejection to the Tlatelpa family's commitment to nurturing their daughters' opportunities and all of the other stories—we witness the profound impact of parental love and support. Each narrative reflects a unique path, yet collectively, they underscore a universal truth: that with unwavering dedication and belief in their children, parents can empower them to surpass expectations and embrace their **limitless future.**

---

80 Anonymous, personal communication, June 2024 (a true story compiled via parent questionnaire).

Nurturing Your Child's Gifts—
It All Begins with You, Parents!

"Our deepest fear is not that we are inadequate. Our deepest fear is that we are powerful beyond measure."
—Marianne Williamson[81]

Every child possesses an exceptional talent, a gift that can flourish and transform into something extraordinary with the right opportunities, experiences, and conditions. As parents, our role is to provide the fertile ground where these gifts can grow, ensuring that children can release the song in them. We parents must believe we are powerful beyond measure to provide the limitless future our children deserve.

Your child's story begins with exposure to opportunities. These opportunities are the gateways to discovery, whether through educational programs, extracurricular activities, volunteering, or new challenges encountered in daily life. Without this exposure, it becomes difficult for children to explore, understand, and discover their varied interests.

Diverse experiences are equally crucial. Various activities allow children to test different fields, skills, and ideas. Each experience is a step toward self-awareness, revealing what excites and motivates them.

---

81 Marianne Williamson, *A Return to Love: Reflections on the Principles of a Course in Miracles*, HarperCollins, 1992.

Through trial and error, children learn what they are passionate about and where their strengths lie.

Central to this is the mindset with which they approach these opportunities. Carol Dweck's concept of a growth mindset is pivotal here. This belief that abilities and intelligence can be developed through dedication and hard work fosters a love for learning and resilience. When children adopt a growth mindset, they are more likely to embrace challenges, persist through setbacks, and view effort as the path to mastery. This attitude is essential for discovering and developing their unique gifts.

Conversely, a fear mindset can hinder this process. Children with a fear mindset may avoid challenges, missing out on experiences that could help them uncover their talents. Overcoming this mindset is crucial for fully exploring and unleashing one's unlimited potential.

Expectations and beliefs also play a significant role. High expectations can drive children to strive for excellence, while low expectations can lead to underachievement. They need to believe in their unlimited potential, a powerful motivator. Viewing mistakes as learning opportunities rather than setbacks is vital. When children understand that failure is not a reflection of their worth but a step toward mastery, they are more likely to persevere and continuously improve.

Realizing their gift involves several key steps. Embracing mistakes as natural parts of the learning process provides valuable lessons and insights. Reflecting on experiences through journaling, mentoring sessions, or thoughtful contemplation helps them recognize patterns, interests, and strengths. Pursuing passions with persistence is crucial, involving continuous learning, practice, and the courage to face and overcome challenges.

Cultivating a supportive environment is equally important. Surrounding children with people who encourage a growth mindset can significantly impact their journey. Mentors, peers, and family who believe in their unlimited potential and provide constructive feedback can be invaluable.

Throughout this book, we've explored the 7 Essential Attributes for children to have a limitless future.

1. **Fostering Persistence:** Encouraging children to keep going, even when faced with obstacles, builds resilience and determination.

2. **Nurturing Precise Communication:** Teaching clear and effective communication helps children express themselves and understand others.

3. **Developing Self-Control:** Instilling self-discipline allows children to manage their impulses and focus on their goals.

4. **Building Empathy:** Cultivating empathy helps children connect with others and fosters a sense of compassion and understanding.

5. **Encouraging Curiosity:** Inspiring a sense of wonder and a desire to learn keeps children engaged and eager to explore new ideas.

6. **Embracing Flexible** Thinking: Promoting adaptability and open-mindedness prepares children to navigate an ever-changing world.

7. **Cultivating Optimism:** Encouraging a positive outlook helps children approach life with hope and confidence, ready to tackle challenges with a constructive mindset.

These attributes are the cornerstones upon which our children can construct a sturdy foundation for lifelong learning, growth, and fulfillment.

Turning a child's interests into a unique gift involves embracing opportunities and diverse experiences, adopting a growth mindset, managing expectations and beliefs, and persistently pursuing passions. By making and learning from mistakes, reflecting on experiences, and cultivating a supportive environment, we can help our children uncover and develop their unique talents, ensuring they never die with their songs still in them. Together, we can nurture their gifts and watch them grow into successful students in school, their chosen fields, and, most importantly, life.

I will end with this question and statement that I posed at the beginning of the book:

What other choice do you have?

Your child can't wait!

Appendix

How Can I Ensure My Child Has a Successful Experience in School Without Relying on the Heroic Efforts of a Single Teacher Like Mrs. Spitz?

In this book, I equip parents with essential tools to understand how the brain functions in the context of learning. I delve into the concepts of growth and fear mindsets and outline seven critical attributes that help foster confidence in children. As a parent, you are Ground Zero; you ignite your child's learning story. You must seek answers, ask questions, and remain informed when encountering unknowns.

In this appendix, I provide a comprehensive set of questions for parents to ask schools, ensuring they are well-informed about contemporary educational practices that support all children, regardless of their background. We must transcend the outdated educational paradigms we experienced and recognize that today's schools should operate significantly differently, informed by the latest research on brain function, learning, and how teachers should work together to ensure the sum is greater than the individual parts.

My esteemed colleague and friend, Rich Smith, an exceptional educator, shares the following narrative. His story about his fifth-grade teacher, Mrs. Spitz, from the 1960s illustrates a dedicated teacher's profound impact on a student's life. Mrs. Spitz was a hero who dramatically altered the course of Rich's life. However, we should not have to rely on individual heroism for our children to have successful, meaningful, and engaging educational experiences. In this appendix, I empower parents with questions to ask schools, ensuring their child has a successful experience every year. Schools must operate as cohesive teams responsible for every child's success.

RICH SMITH—IN HIS OWN WORDS

Why am I in this business? My mom was 16 when she met my dad. He was 19. They got married, and my mom had me before her 17th birthday. By the time my mom was 23, she had five kids. My mom is from West Virginia; she didn't graduate from high school until she was 39. My dad is from Oklahoma, near Broken Arrow. He barely graduated from high school. When they first got married, they moved to the East Bay, the East Bay of San Francisco, and we lived in a very tough neighborhood.

My mom didn't know much about anything, including sending me to school. A man came to the house and said, "Ma'am, you've got to have your kid in school." So, as a six-year-old, they sent me to first grade, skipping kindergarten. I started in the Bluebird reading group, the top group, but was quickly moved to the Buzzard group, a group of one, where I struggled. By second grade, I was still in the Buzzard group. I started with ten spelling words, then eight, then six, and eventually none.

In third grade, things got much more difficult, and I cried a lot because I couldn't read. On the last day of school, my teacher wrote on my report card "Richie is a very nice boy, but he's not college material." This was 1963, and kids were being divided into college-bound and blue-collar groups. I was clearly in the latter.

Fourth grade wasn't much better. I spent most of my time sweeping hallways or serving food in the cafeteria. On the last day, I received a card indicating my next teacher. I couldn't read it, so I asked a kid, who told me, "You have Mrs. Spitz." Mrs. Spitz was a small woman who always wore a white blouse, black skirt, and square-heeled shoes. She resembled the Wicked Witch of the West. I dreaded going to her class.

On the first day of fifth grade, my mom walked me to school and stood with me in line. Mrs. Spitz came out and said, "Come on in, have a seat. You're going to learn a lot this year, work hard, and do what I say." Within five minutes, we were working, and I was a mess because I couldn't read. She kept telling me, "You'll learn. You'll be done when you're done."

Every day at 3:00, when the other kids left, Mrs. Spitz would keep me and a few others behind to complete our work. I stayed after school until 6:30, Monday through Friday, until January. I hated her with a passion. By February, I was going home earlier and earlier, and by the end of the year, I could read and went home at 3:00 with the other kids.

Mrs. Spitz saw a poor, struggling kid and decided to make a difference. I wouldn't be here if it weren't for her. Because of her, I have a wife, a career, and a successful family. My daughter is a designer in Los Angeles, my son graduated from the Air Force Academy and works as an engineer, and my other son is an economist at the Air Force Academy. All of this is because of a teacher who saw my worth and made a difference in my life.

As a teacher, I often heard Mrs. Spitz's voice coming out of my mouth. I cried at her funeral, regretting that I never shared the difference she made in my life. Kids sometimes snarl or push back, but they need you to believe in them and make a difference in their lives. Many of us are here because someone believed in us.

I often think about how if Mrs. Spitz had shared her knowledge with other teachers, I might not have had to stay after school until 6:30. I could have been helped much earlier. A teacher with that much knowledge needs to share it with others. We work in the greatest profession in the world, one that changes not just today but the future. God bless you for being in this profession.

–Rich Smith

In the entire speech about Mrs. Spitz, the first two sentences in the last paragraph are the most important for you to know about as parents. Rich speaks to the heart of exactly how schools should operate today, where teachers should abandon the idea of being isolated classroom teachers in favor of teams of teachers who take collective responsibility for every single child. As you read the following questions, think about how you are framing them as if a team of teachers and the entire school are taking collective responsibility for your child and how that school is working to ensure they are doing so.

How Does the School Support Fostering Confidence in My Child with the 7 Essential Attributes?

1. Persistence: How does the school encourage and support students to develop persistence, especially when faced with challenging tasks or setbacks? Are specific programs or activities designed to help children build and practice this attribute? Additionally, does your staff participate in professional learning opportunities focused on growth, fear, and fixed mindsets?

2. Precise Communication: What strategies or practices does the school employ to enhance students' precise communication skills? Can you provide examples of how students are taught to express their thoughts clearly and listen actively?

3. Self-Control: How does the school help students develop self-control? Are there any techniques or classroom management strategies used to teach children how to regulate their emotions and behaviors effectively?

4. Empathy: How does the school foster empathy among students? Are there programs or initiatives that encourage students to understand

and share the feelings of others, such as peer mentoring or community service projects?

5. Curiosity: What opportunities does the school provide to nurture and stimulate students' curiosity? Are there specific subjects, projects, or extracurricular activities designed to encourage exploration and a love of learning?

6. Flexible Thinking: How does the school promote flexible thinking and adaptability in students? Do activities or lessons challenge students to think creatively and consider multiple perspectives when solving problems?

7. Optimism: How does the school cultivate optimism in students? Are there practices that help students develop a positive outlook, resilience, and the ability to see challenges as opportunities for growth?

What Strategies Can Educators Use That Have Traditionally Been Reserved for Students Labeled as Gifted but Should Be Used for All Students in My Child's School?

After reading this book, especially Chapter 1, and understanding how the brain affects learning and how growth mindset and fear mindsets can help anyone grow intelligence, you should understand that every child is born a genius.

Throughout my career, I've observed different educational methods educators utilize that benefit students. Often, I found myself implementing approaches that felt right, even without full awareness of their research or specific names. Transitioning into an administrative role allowed me to delve deeper into various approaches and identify them precisely. Influential figures like Gholdy Muhammad, Carol Ann Tomlinson, Yvette Jackson, and Zaretta Hammond have written about approaches aligning with my beliefs. Some strategies in this section are adapted from their work, shaping my perspective on effective educational methods.[82]

In Chapter 4 of *Every Student Deserves a Gifted Education*, I outline 7 Powerful Strategies for Educators to provide any student with a gifted experience:

1. **Harvesting Student Strengths and Centering Student Perspectives**

2. **Fostering Connections and Connecting Learning**

3. **Elevating High Cognitive Performance**

4. **Offering Enhanced Learning Experiences**

5. **Identifying Prerequisites to Ensure Learning**

6. **Acknowledging Different Points of Entry into the Curriculum**

7. **Creating a Flexible Classroom**

Fostering critical and creative thinking through various techniques, such as Literature Circles, Document-Based Questions (DBQ), De Bono's Thinking Hats, and Socratic seminars, Project-Based Learning (PBL) are experiences that any student should be able to participate in.

While this brief overview provides insight into what every school should do to offer gifted experiences to all children, I urge you to advocate for these strategies actively. Consider purchasing *Every Student Deserves a Gifted Education* and *sharing it with your child's school*. By doing so, you can help ensure that they adopt strategies and practices traditionally only provided to students with a gifted and talented label,

---

82 Adapted from *Every Student Deserves a Gifted Education*, 2023, p. 145.

which should benefit all students.

Questions for Parents Regarding a
Multi-Tiered System of Support (MTSS)

My Child Is Struggling With a Skill or Concept... What Next?

My Child Has Mastered a Skill or Concept... What Next?

1. How do you identify if a child needs extra help or advanced challenges?

Can you give an example of this process?

The kind of answer I should expect from the school below:

We assess students through our frequent common formative assessments and teacher observations. For example, if a student consistently masters specific skills or concepts at grade level, we may consider advanced challenges.

2. What criteria do you use to decide on extra support or advanced challenges?

Can you show me an example?

The kind of answer I should expect from the school below:

We consider multiple factors, such as lack of mastery or mastery of grade-level essential skills. For example, if a student consistently struggles to grasp certain concepts like inferring in reading or 2 × 2 multiplication, we may provide extra help. If they master that grade-level essential skill faster, we will extend or deepen their learning to challenge them further.

3. How often do you review and update my child's progress?

Can you provide a recent example?

The kind of answer I should expect from the school below:

We check on your student's progress on essential curriculum frequently based on the individual and team support depending on our weekly data from our checks for understanding and standard formative assessment process. For example, if a student's needs change or there's a significant shift in academic performance, we'll adjust the plan at our weekly or biweekly team meetings. Individual teachers have the flexibility within their class to adjust minute by minute if, through their assessments, they see the need to adjust.

4. Does my child have access to the essential grade-level curriculum? Can you show me how this is provided in class?

The kind of answer I should expect from the school below:

Yes, all students have access to the essential **grade-level curriculum.** If your child needs support with **pre-requisite skills** to access grade-level content and **foundation skills,** they will also receive that support. It's not either-or; they will receive all three levels of support.

5. What specific supports or strategies are used to help my child succeed?

Can you give examples?

The kind of answer I should expect from the school below:

Interventions are based on needs from assessments, observations, and our teacher team discussions. They are targeted to the specific behaviors or academic skills/standards that the student needs support with. For example, if a student **struggles with organization**, we may provide daily check-ins and assistance in setting goals. Another example is if a student has **difficulty identifying the parts of a story**, such as character, setting, problem, or solution, that will be targeted. In **physical education**, if they can't dribble a ball with their opposite hand, they will receive targeted extra time and support in that area. Interventions and extensions are for every subject area, and your child should benefit from these supports no matter who the teacher is.

6. How do you ensure the core teaching methods work for most students, including those like my child?
Can you show data or examples?

The kind of answer I should expect from the school below:

We regularly assess the effectiveness of our teaching methods through data analysis and feedback from the assessments. For example, suppose one teacher shows to be more effective at teaching a skill than their colleagues based on the common assessment they gave. In that case, that colleague will share and model teaching strategies with their colleagues to support their improvement in teaching that skill.

7. When was my child identified for extra support, and what process was used?

Can you provide an example of the timeline and process?

The kind of answer I should expect from the school below:

Your child was identified for extra support [specific time], following [specific processes such as assessments or teacher observations]. For example, if a student consistently struggled with math concepts, we conducted diagnostic assessments to pinpoint areas of difficulty.

8. What are my child's specific learning or behavioral needs that prompted extra support?

Can you show how these needs are documented and addressed?

The kind of answer I should expect from the school below:

Your child's needs include [specific needs such as difficulty with reading comprehension or difficulty focusing]. We document these needs through assessments, teacher observations, and input from parents. For example, if a student has difficulty focusing, we collaborate as a teacher team and staff and communicate with parents on an ongoing basis to develop strategies to support their learning in the classroom.

9. How do you monitor my child's progress and make adjustments?

Can you show examples of progress reports and adjustments made?

The kind of answer I should expect from the school below:

We monitor your child's progress through [specific methods such as regular assessments or progress monitoring tools]. For example, we use weekly progress reports to track academic performance and behavior. If we notice any areas of concern, we collaborate as a teacher team and staff and communicate with parents continuously to make necessary adjustments to support their child's success.

10. Will my child be removed from special classes like art, music, physical education, band, etc., if they struggle to get more support in reading and math?

The kind of answer I should expect from the school below:

No! We have a coordinated Multi-Tiered System of Support for both Interventions and Extensions in which your child should receive additional help without missing classes that are as important to their interest and development as math and reading.

P.S. Although these questions are a starting point and can assist you in getting initial information and answers from your child's school, *Taking Action* (2ⁿᵈ Edition) is the most comprehensive book that I know of on this subject. See Recommended Resources at the end of the Appendix.

JUST BECAUSE I FOUND THIS STUDY INTERESTING

Understanding How Knowledge Components and Extensive Practice Lead to Mastery

In the study *An Astonishing Regularity in Student Learning Rate* by Kenneth R. Koedinger et al. (2023), the researchers analyzed data from twenty-seven studies in academic settings. They found that everyone needs extensive practice to become proficient, typically around seven opportunities per component of knowledge. A ***knowledge component*** is a discrete unit of knowledge or skill that can be learned and mastered independently, such as understanding how to add fractions in mathematics, playing a specific chord in music, or mastering a particular dribbling technique in basketball.

Additionally, the researchers discovered that there are no substantial differences in the rate at which individuals learn. They suggested that these findings challenge existing learning theories and highlight the importance of providing equal learning opportunities to reduce educational achievement gaps.[83]

---

83 Kenneth R. Koedinger et al, "An Astonishing Regularity in Student Learning Rate," *Proceedings of the National Academy of Sciences*, March 2023, 120(13): e2221311120.

How Parents Can Use This
Information to Help Their Children

1. Create Practice Opportunities: Ensure your child gets plenty of practice for each knowledge component they are learning. For example, if they are learning multiplication, provide exercises that allow them to practice regularly. If they are learning to play the piano, ensure they have opportunities to practice scales and chords consistently.

2. Consistent Practice: Recognize that becoming proficient in any skill or knowledge area requires repeated practice. Encourage your child to practice regularly rather than cramming all at once.

3. Provide Targeted Feedback: As your child practices, offer specific, constructive feedback on their performance. This helps them understand what they are doing well and what needs improvement, facilitating more effective learning.

4. Encourage Access to Varied Learning Opportunities and Experiences: Support and ensure your child's access to a diverse array of learning resources and experiences. Offer them books across different genres, educational tools tailored to their interests, musical instruments representing various cultures and genres, and a spectrum of healthy hobbies such as sports, chess, the arts, outdoor activities, and more. Exposing your child to a broad range of opportunities and experiences enables them to explore and uncover their passions and interests.

5. Track Progress: Monitor your child's progress in different areas to ensure they are getting enough practice opportunities and support where needed.

6. Encourage Persistence: Help your child understand that needing multiple attempts to master something is normal. Encourage them to persist and reassure them that everyone learns at their own pace, but with consistent effort, they will succeed.

Examples of Knowledge Components

Music: Learning to play a specific chord on the guitar or piano. Each chord represents a knowledge component that, once mastered, contributes to the ability to play a song.

Sports: In basketball, mastering a dribbling technique or a specific type of shot. Each method or shot is a knowledge component that, once practiced and perfected, enhances overall performance in the game.

Some children may become proficient more quickly around a specific knowledge component because they have already acquired other prerequisite or foundational skills related to that knowledge component, while others have not. These prerequisite skills could have been obtained through various opportunities afforded to them, such as prior lessons, extracurricular activities, or enriched environments. Once all students have these prerequisite and foundational skills, the amount of practice required to master new skills is the same for everyone.

Understanding variations in learning pace is crucial, as some students may demonstrate accelerated learning due to their pre-existing interest and relevance in specific knowledge components. For instance, a child might grasp multiplication concepts faster because they find math intriguing and applicable to their interests, while another child, lacking similar enthusiasm, may require more time and effort to comprehend the same material. This discrepancy in engagement level can significantly influence the amount of effort students invest in practice, ultimately affecting their learning outcomes. Therefore, acknowledging and catering to individual interests and relevance can be pivotal in optimizing engagement and effort and facilitating more efficient learning experiences.

Moreover, when parents recognize their child's intrinsic motivation and relevance toward specific knowledge components, they can tailor practice opportunities accordingly, capitalizing on the child's natural curiosity and passion. By aligning practice activities with their child's interests, parents can enhance engagement, increase motivation, and foster a deeper understanding of the subject matter. This personalized approach promotes efficient learning and cultivates a positive attitude toward continuous self-improvement, laying the foundation for lifelong learning and success.[84]

EMBRACING INNOVATIVE EDUCATIONAL PRINCIPLES— AN INSPIRATIONAL SCHOOL

In the introduction, I wrote about Dr. George Land's study in which he found that 98 percent of five-year-olds started as geniuses. Still, he pointed a finger at traditional schooling as to why most lost their genius status by the time they reached adulthood. As I pointed out in my book *Every Student Deserves a Gifted Education*, some inspirational schools and districts embrace Dr. Land's belief that every child starts as a genius and support teaching the growth mindset philosophy. A school that I did not highlight in *Every Student Deserves a Gifted Education* that deserves much attention is The Village School in Arlington, Virginia, founded by an amazing forward-thinking educator, Lauren Quinn.[85] The Village School is designed around three essential pillars to give children agency in their learning: Learner-Centered, Play-Based, and Character-Based education.

---

84 *Proceedings of the National Academy of Sciences*, a peer-reviewed journal of the National Academy of Sciences, https://www.pnas.org, accessed on May 6, 2024.
85 The Village School, https://www.villageschoolnova.org/.

The Village School focuses on creating self-directed learners who can lead themselves and their communities. Rather than adhering to a rigid, one-size-fits-all curriculum, the school respects each child's unique path to growth. This is achieved through flexible learning plans, allowing children to set, pursue, and accomplish their goals. Supported by dedicated guides, students work on mastering fundamental skills like reading, writing, and math while also exploring their passions. This approach ensures that each child's learning journey is personalized and deeply engaging.

Playful learning is integral to The Village School's daily routine, benefiting learners of all ages. Research consistently shows play's profound learning and social benefits, yet traditional classrooms often stifle this natural curiosity. At The Village School, play and creative, hands-on projects are central to the learning experience. Students immerse themselves in real-world activities, from unstructured play and launching start-up businesses to programming robots and gardening. Each activity encourages problem-solving, experimentation, and reflection, helping students develop practical skills and a lifelong love of learning.

The Village School believes who its learners become is more important than what they know. Viewing each student as trustworthy, capable, and kind, the school aims to profoundly impact their self-worth and development. The school's learning design intentionally fosters opportunities for children to think independently, make sound decisions, and respect others' opinions and ideas. By nurturing these character traits, The Village School helps students grow into well-rounded individuals ready to contribute positively to their communities.

Although The Village School is a private institution, these principles should be embraced by both public and private schools alike. By doing so, we can ensure that each child's limitless potential is unleashed, fostering a generation of confident, capable, independent, and compassionate individuals.

Adaptation of Powerful Quotes from David Shenk's Book *The Genius in All of Us* (2010)

I want to end this section with an adaptation and summary of the quotes that introduce each chapter in David Shenk's book *The Genius in All of Us*. Understanding what is possible for our children is crucial for us to believe in their limitless potential to achieve great things, regardless of their starting point or the challenges they may face. When children are genuinely interested and engaged, they can surpass our expectations. Take a moment to read, reflect, and challenge any long-held assumptions or limiting beliefs about what our children can achieve. Often, we unknowingly restrict a child's possibilities based on our own experiences, beliefs, lack of understanding, misinterpretation, or the influence of those around us who also lack awareness of the latest research and evidence on learning and achievement. These quotes highlight the dynamic interaction between genes and environment, debunking some long-held beliefs and emphasizing the enormous potential for growth and development in every individual.

Contrary to the traditional belief that genes alone determine physical and character traits, Shenk asserts that these traits result from an intricate interaction between genes and the environment. This dynamic and ongoing process continually refines an individual, emphasizing that our genetic code is not a fixed blueprint but a flexible script that adapts and evolves with our experiences.

Intelligence is not a fixed attribute encoded at birth. Instead, it is a collection of developing skills driven by the interplay between genes and the environment. Shenk argues that no one is born with a predetermined amount of intelligence; it can be cultivated and improved. Alfred Binet, the inventor of the original IQ test, passionately opposed the idea that intelligence is unchangeable,

advocating instead for the potential for growth and improvement in every individual.

Like intelligence, talents are not innate gifts but the result of a gradual accumulation of skills developed from conception onward. While everyone is born with unique differences and some advantages for certain tasks, greatness is not genetically predetermined. Few are biologically restricted from attaining significant achievements, highlighting the potential within each person to develop their abilities through persistent effort and favorable conditions.

Identical twins often display striking similarities, but these arise from more than just their genetic profiles. Their differences, often overlooked, illustrate the profound influence of environmental factors. Twin studies, widely misinterpreted, reveal that genetic influence is not direct and fixed. Instead, these studies highlight the significant role of environment and individual experiences in shaping potential.

Child prodigies and superlative adult achievers are often not the same individuals. Understanding the emergence of remarkable abilities at different life stages provides crucial insights into the nature of talent. This distinction emphasizes that talent is a developmental process, not a static trait.

Ethnic and geographical clusters of athletic success often prompt suspicions of hidden genetic advantages. However, the real advantages are more nuanced and less related to specific genes. Research suggests that racial and ethnic groups are not genetically discrete, with genetic variation within populations far exceeding differences between them. Athletic potential is widespread and influenced by a complex interplay of genes and environmental factors.

The traditional nature vs. nurture paradigm is flawed. Shenk argues that we have more control over our genes and less control over our environment than commonly believed. This book is not about finding hidden geniuses but about recognizing the buildable and developing nature of human potential. It dismantles the myth of innate giftedness, showing that ordinary people can achieve extraordinary things through effort and opportunity.

Parenting plays a crucial role in nurturing children's potential. There are many ways parents can encourage their kids to become achievers, and it is equally important to avoid certain mistakes. Effective parenting involves fostering an environment that supports growth and learning.

Fostering greatness should not be left to genes and parents alone. Society also has a responsibility to spur individual achievement. Cultures must strive to promote values that bring out the best in people, and Shenk's 7 Essential Attributes aim to create a supportive environment for excellence.

Epigenetics introduces the concept of free will into our understanding of genetics. According to Randall Jirtle from Duke University, lifestyle choices can affect gene expression and the heredity of future generations. This discovery revolutionizes our understanding of disease, human abilities, and evolution, demonstrating that lifestyle can indeed alter heredity.[86]

Possible Opportunities and Experiences for Your Child[87]

These are some of the specific activities and opportunities from the "Inspiring the Future: Nurturing Kindness, Community, and Lifelong Learning" story in Chapter 9, which Lindsay and Sam experienced from when they were born until they were five.

---

86 David Shenk, *The Genius in All of Us: New Insights into Genetics, Talents, and IQ.* Anchor Books, 2010.
87 Adapted from internet search and parent survey.

Lindsay

Bilingual Preschool: Spanish Montessori School

Parent and Me Activities: gymnastics and swim lessons

Art and Culture: art classes at the community center, travel to museums and field trips (including the Mexican Embassy), Legoland, zoos, aquariums

Sports and Recreation: soccer, tee-ball, ballet, martial arts, swim lessons

Family Activities: eating at the dinner table, cooking classes, frequent park/playground days, playdates with friends, family, and neighbors

Special Outings: amusement parks, fall festivals, farm visits, beach trips, Disneyland, Disney World, cruises

Learning and Development: early intervention with a child psychologist, bookstores, indoor play spaces, national park visits, pottery classes, science camp, plays, Cirque Du Soleil

Home Life: regularly cooking/baking with mom and dad, Kiwi Crate subscription, frequent library trips and story time events, reading at bedtime, developmentally appropriate chore charts

Health and Traditions: regular visits with the pediatrician, holiday traditions (cutting down Christmas trees, viewing Christmas lights, stringing popcorn, etc.), large birthday parties that include people from all our spheres

Parental Education: we read much literature about raising children and supporting emotional growth

Sam

Preschool: part-day preschool at the school district

Parenting Approach: I stayed home much longer before returning to work, working only part-time and then from home

Parent and Me Activities: gymnastics and swim classes

Art and Culture: travel to museums, Legoland, zoos, aquariums

Sports and Recreation: soccer, tee-ball, swim lessons

Family Activities: gardening, eating dinner at the table, frequent park/playground days, playdates with friends, family, and neighbors

Special Outings: amusement parks, fall festivals, farm visits

Learning and Development: 4H involvement, early reading intervention, tagging along during older sister's homeschool events, playing video games with dad

Home Life: regularly cooks with his parents, developmentally appropriate chore chart, Kiwi Crate subscription, reading at bedtime, frequent library trips and story time events, regular well visits with the pediatrician, summer reading programs at the library

Health and Traditions: state fair, holiday traditions (cutting down Christmas tree, viewing Christmas lights, stringing popcorn, etc.), large birthday parties that include all people in our orbit, traveling (Disney cruise)

Other Possible Opportunities for Parents and Children

1. Parent-Child Classes: Enroll in parent-child classes like music and movement, sensory play, or baby yoga, which provide opportunities for bonding and development in a supportive environment.

2. Early Literacy Programs: Participate in early literacy programs at libraries or community centers, including story time sessions, puppet shows, and interactive storytelling activities.

3. Parent-Child Groups: Join groups where caregivers and children engage in activities like playdates, sing-alongs, and sensory exploration.

4. Playgroups: Attend playgroups where children can socialize, learn to share and take turns, and engage in age-appropriate play activities with peers.

5. Baby Sign Language Classes: Enroll in baby sign language classes to facilitate early communication and language development for pre-verbal infants and toddlers.

6. Parenting Workshops: Attend parenting workshops or support groups focusing on child development, positive discipline, and early childhood education.

7. Early Intervention Services: Access early intervention services for children with developmental delays or disabilities, including screenings, assessments, and therapies tailored to individual needs.

8. Music Classes: Enroll in music classes designed specifically for infants and toddlers. These classes incorporate singing, movement, and exposure to different musical instruments.

9. Outdoor Playgroups: Join outdoor or nature-based programs where children can explore outdoor environments, engage in sensory experiences, and learn about nature.

10. Art and Sensory Exploration: Provide opportunities for art and sensory exploration at home through finger painting, playdough play, and sensory bins with various textures and materials.

11. Gymnastics or Movement Classes: Enroll in gymnastics or movement classes focusing on developing gross motor skills, coordination, and body awareness through age-appropriate activities.

12. Infant Massage Classes: Participate in infant massage classes to learn techniques for bonding, relaxation, and promoting healthy development in babies.

13. Storytelling and Rhyme Time: Engage in storytelling sessions and rhyme time activities at home or in community settings to promote language development, vocabulary, and listening skills.

14. Baby Gymnastics: Attend baby gymnastics classes, which offer gentle exercises, stretching, and movement activities to support infants' physical development and coordination.

15. Parent-Child Swim Classes: Participate in parent-child swim classes where caregivers and children can bond while learning water safety skills and basic swimming techniques.

16. Library Programs: Take advantage of library programs such as "Books for Babies" and "Toddlers Time" that offer early literacy activities, songs, and stories tailored to young children.

17. Sensory Playdates: Arrange sensory playdates with other families to allow children to explore different sensory materials and experiences in a social setting.

18. Baby and Me Yoga: Join baby and me yoga classes, which incorporate gentle yoga poses, stretches, and relaxation techniques for caregivers and infants to enjoy together.

19. Babywearing Groups: Join babywearing groups or meetups where caregivers can learn about and practice using baby carriers while bonding with their infants.

20. Outdoor Exploration: Take children on outdoor excursions to parks, playgrounds, and nature reserves, allowing them to explore and interact with their environment while developing gross motor skills and curiosity.

21. Preschools are crucial in preparing children for kindergarten and beyond by providing a structured learning environment that fosters cognitive, social, and emotional development.[88]

Where Can I Find Out About These Opportunities?

1. YMCA (Young Men's Christian Association): The YMCA typically offers a range of family programs, including parent-child classes, swim lessons, sports leagues, and childcare services.

2. Local Parks and Recreation Departments: Many local parks and recreation departments organize parent-child classes, playgroups, and family events such as nature walks, arts and crafts workshops, and outdoor festivals.

3. Parenting Centers or Family Resource Centers: These centers often provide support, education, and resources for parents and families, including parenting classes, playgroups, and early childhood development programs.

4. Early Childhood Education Centers or Preschools: Some early childhood education centers or preschools offer parent-child classes, family events, and workshops focused on child development and parenting skills.

---

88 Adapted from internet search and parent survey.

5. Children's Museums: Children's museums frequently host family-friendly exhibits, workshops, and events to engage young children and their caregivers in hands-on learning and exploration.

6. Local Libraries: Public libraries often offer early literacy programs, story time sessions, and workshops for parents and caregivers, as well as access to children's books, educational toys, and resources.

7. Family Support Organizations: Nonprofit organizations focused on family support and early childhood development may offer various programs and services, including parenting classes, playgroups, and support groups for parents.

8. Community Health Centers: Some community health centers or clinics offer parenting classes, child development screenings, and support services for families with young children.

9. Cultural Centers and Ethnic Community Organizations: Cultural centers and organizations may host cultural events, festivals, and activities for families, providing opportunities for children to learn about their heritage and cultural traditions.

10. Churches, Synagogues, Mosques, or Religious Institutions: Religious institutions often offer family-friendly activities, parenting classes, and support groups, as well as childcare services and programs for young children.

11. Preschools: Parents can research and inquire about preschools in their local area to find the best fit for their child's needs and interests.

12. Salvation Army Boys and Girls Club[89]

---

89 Adapted from internet search and parent survey.

These organizations represent valuable resources for families with young children, providing opportunities for learning, support, and community engagement.

Recommended Resources to Support Your Child's School

- *Every Student Deserves a Gifted Education* by Brian Butler
- *What About Us? The PLC at Work Process for Grades PreK-2 Teams* by Kerr, Heller, Hulen, and Butler
- *Ruthless Equity* by Ken Williams
- *15-Day Challenge* by Maria Nielsen
- *Mindset: The New Psychology of Success* by Carol Dweck
- *Cultivating Genius* by Gholdy Muhammad
- *The Pedagogy of Confidence* by Yvette Jackson
- *Taking Action* (2nd Edition) by Mattos, Buffum, Malone, Cruz, Schuhl, and Dimich
- *Learning by Doing* (4th Edition) by DuFour, DuFour, Eaker, Many, Mattos, and Muhammad
- *Time for Change* by Anthony Muhammad and Luis Cruz
- *Literacy in a PLC at Work* by Paula Maeker and Jacqueline Heller
- *Building Blocks for Social Emotional Learning* by Ann-Bailey Lipsett and Tracey Hulen
- *The Genius in All of Us* by David Shenk

Acknowledgments

This book is a testament to the unwavering support of my wife, Kathleen Bragaw, who encouraged me to begin writing after I did not think I could get this project done, and for that, I am eternally grateful. To my daughters, Alison and Emily, you embody the 7 Essential Attributes explored in this book. Your lives, filled with honor, humility, and determination, were a constant inspiration throughout this journey.

I am profoundly thankful to the reviewers who generously offered their time to provide insightful feedback that elevated the quality of *Limitless Future*. Thanks to Karen Olweiler, Bernard Jones, Nikki Heinlein, Sue Morgan, and Noelle Klein for your invaluable contributions.

To the parents who participated in the survey, your stories and perspectives were instrumental in shaping the content of this book. My deepest gratitude goes to Angela Samosorn, Juana Tlatelpa, Alisha Davidson, Dan Redding, Ann-Bailey Lipsett, and Patty Edwards.

I also want to acknowledge my accountability partners. Your willingness to receive my texts and emails during the writing process kept me grounded and motivated. Thank you, Diane Kerr, Jacquie Heller, Mike Mattos, Doug Gee, Ken Williams, Mike Brown, Ashley Friend, Tracey Hulen, John and Jessica Hannigan, Robyn Dawson, Nicole Dimich, Mark Ausbrooks, Cassie Guy, Nicole Walker, Craig Helms, Charles Brooks, Lillie Jessie, Lori Noble O'Malley (whose thought-provoking question sparked the creation of this book), Mark Esherick, Nicole Wozniak, Chris Jerry, Willie Benton, Jenn Deinhart, Clara Sale-Davis, Maria Nielsen, Geri Parscale, Paula Maeker, Gavin Grift, Blake Cates,

Marguarite Gooden, Lindsay Eck, Louise Robertson, Paula Rogers, Rich Smith, Peggy Holder, and Jeff Craig.

I want to thank my book publishing team, Martha Bullen, my wonderful book coach and consultant; Christy Day, my interior designer and cover designer, for the amazing job she and her team have done; and Dave Aretha, my editor, for his excellence and efficient work. Publishing a book is a team effort, and I am honored to have the best people working to make my book worth the read.

A special thank you to Lauren Quinn for allowing me to share the story of her wonderful school, The Village School, which is an inspiring example of what is possible when we nurture every child's limitless potential.

Finally, to the endorsers who believed in this work and its potential to make a difference for parents: Mike Durso, Bernard Jones, Suzanne Morgan, Nikki Heinlein, Noelle Klein, Karen Olweiler, Byron Kerr & Lisa Wolfe, and Floyd Wilson. Your support means the world to me.

About the Author

BRIAN BUTLER is an educational consultant, speaker, author, and award-winning former principal who is passionate about nurturing collaborative school cultures that unlock every student's unlimited potential. Brian has advised thousands of schools across the United States, Australia, and Canada.

As a former school-based educator and principal, Brian worked with countless parents and parent groups, supporting and guiding them in their essential role in nurturing their children's growth and potential. He emphasized the importance of leveraging the unique strengths and insights that each family contributed. Brian's goal is to help parents recognize that they hold the key to their children's success and development, which drove him throughout his career to create a collaborative and empowering environment so every child could flourish.

Brian is the author of *Limitless Future: An Action Guide to Nurturing Your Child's Unique Strengths, Passions, and Talents* and *Every Student Deserves a Gifted Education: 5 Shifts to Nurturing Each Student's Unique Strengths, Passions, and Talents*. He is also co-author of *What About Us?*

The PLC at Work Process for Grades PreK-2 Teams and a contributing author of *It's About Time: Planning Interventions and Extensions in Elementary Schools.*

Brian has enjoyed diverse career experiences, including being a professional basketball player in the European League. He holds a bachelor's degree in speech communications from The George Washington University, a teacher's certification in physical education, and a master's degree in school counseling from George Mason University. With an administrative endorsement from the University of Virginia, Brian is known for his ability to drive positive change.

Beyond his professional achievements, Brian and his wife Kathleen are proud parents to two adult daughters, Alison and Emily. Brian and Kathleen live in northern Virginia. To learn more or contact Brian, visit.brianbutler.info.